Hi Insecurity. Insecurity.

Hi Insecurity. BYE Insecurity.

BY

SHAUNEE BRANNAN

Published by
Prayers and Punchlines, LLC
Detroit, MI

ISBN 978-1-5136-1872-2

DEDICATIONS

This book is dedicated to my parents, Edmond and Towana Parker. The older I get, the more I realize what a gift you two are in my life. Without your love, encouragement, admonition, and support, I wouldn't have gotten as far as I have. My goal is to make you even prouder than you are, and to prove that every sacrifice you all have ever made for your children, were seeds planted into our future, and seeds into your futures as well. Your best days are ahead of you both. Each of you are my heroes.

I would also like to dedicate this body of work to my husband, Gayle, who has always encouraged and supported my gift. Gayle, you were one of the first people to recognize my gift, and to help give me the theological context and spiritual guidance necessary to grow. You have never placed boundaries on the ministry God has given me. You have allowed me to work alongside you; you have not treated me as a subordinate, but an equal. How you've helped me, speaks volumes about your security in God and your belief in who I am. I love you.

Finally, I would like to dedicate this book to my daughters, Haven and Cadence. Long after I am gone, and the two of you have families of your own, my prayer is that everything I've ever taught you pertaining to your worth and value, rings ever true, as it is all reiterated on these pages. When in doubt, read the words on these pages. When you miss me, read them. When you are afraid, read them. Read them until you know them by heart. Once you've both done this, pass the book down to your children, letting them know that this is part of their legacy. Mommy loves you both beyond imagination.

RECOMMENDATION

When my wife asked me to write the recommendation for her book, I was not only honored, but thought to myself: *This will be extremely easy to write being that I know her intimately.* On a personal level, I know what God has done and is doing in my wife. Having been married for some time now, I have both profited, and been amazed at the wisdom and insight that God has entrusted to her. Not only is she a woman of God, but she has a heart of compassion for people who struggle with insecurity and, like most of us, has wrestled with it herself. I have heard several people over the years say to me that they love the confidence they see in their encounters with Shaunee. Knowing her the way I do now, I can testify that her confidence is the direct result of submitting to a relationship with God. The truth is, God always wants us to perceive ourselves the way He perceives us. I highly recommend this book for both men and women. This book is loaded with revelation that will help all who read, overcome one of the enemy's most deceptive weapons, which is insecurity. It has been my privilege to be married to a woman of God that not only flows in revelation, but also lives with integrity.

Pastor Gayle Brannan, Jr.

ACKNOWLEDGEMENTS

This is my first venture of this nature, and it would have never been possible without the many resources I've pulled from for advice, correction, and assistance. Thank you all for your time, consideration, and love.

Gayle Brannan, thank you for writing my Recommendation. You are such a brilliant and critical thinker. I am honored to have continual access to your intellect and wisdom. You go against the grain, and for that, there is no box that can confine you.

Bishop Ken Shelton, thank you for taking the time to write my Foreword, and for all the times you have been there for Gayle and me. You are a Godsend; we respect you so much. You are by far one of the wisest men we know.

Bishop Jamie Englehart, thank you for your quote and for the relationship you have with our ministry. We have learned so much from you and appreciate your love for us.

Apostle Tony Howson, thank you for years of being available to Gayle and me. For quite some time, you have watched us evolve. Your contribution as it pertains to this book, was confirmation and affirmation. Your heart for God and love for people, are the qualities I admire most in you.

Teachia Turrentine, thank you for your diligence and patience in editing this book. I thought I was an English guru, until you got ahold of a few chapters and showed me what a guru really is. I love your heart for God, and I love how you're able to help me look even smarter, without losing my heart in it all. I look forward to everything God has for you. You're a diamond.

Beverly Dobrich, thank you for your prayers, advice, and help with this lengthy process. The resources you've provided have helped steer me in the right direction, leaving no stone unturned.

No, I'm not done yet.

To my siblings, Tanaya Parker, Edmond Parker, Jr., and Gabriel Parker, thank you all for your love and encouragement.

Chantele Gray, Kelli Brownlee, Iantha Lane, and Marlania Brown, my friends, thank you all for remaining true to who you are throughout the years. Thank you for admonishing me. Thank you for believing in me. Thank you for telling me to, in so many words, "go for it." You each defy all the negative stereotypes regarding women in relationships. You all are blessings to my life.

Lastly, thank you to my church family, Vertical Encounter Church. You all have always supported and encouraged my gift. You accept me as I am, making no distinction in respect between Gayle and me, but acknowledging our oneness. You are the best and most loving group of people. I know that if I'm never accepted or welcomed anywhere else, I'd be just fine. The acceptance I have from you all, is more than enough.

FOREWORD

Having known Shaunee Brannan for at least a decade, it was enlightening for me to read her personal stories about insecurity. If a stranger asked me to describe her, I would use the following adjectives: outgoing, talented, attractive, strong, smart, and confident. Over time, I have become even more convinced that she possesses these attributes. This is one reason why this book is so important. It is more than another book on personal development. *Hi Insecurity. BYE Insecurity.*, is a real-life story.

It is entirely possible to build a powerful exterior and hide an insecure interior. Most of us have experienced this reality to some degree. Without the help of someone who is also traveling the road of personal uncertainty, it is difficult to make real progress. It takes courage to unzip your skin and show others what is going on inside, which is exactly what the author has done.

A gifted teacher will not only give out information, she will also give readers the tools necessary to identify their own issues, and practical steps toward recovery. Yes, this book shares some very personal stories; however, the author has also provided opportunities for personal reflection and workbook assignments with insightful questions, to jumpstart you on your path to growth and overcoming insecurity.

Shaunee Brannan is more than a writer, she is a daughter, a sister, a wife, a mother, an account executive, a powerful vocalist and worship leader, but she is also a pastor. Shaunee and her husband, Gayle Brannan, Jr., serve as lead pastors at Vertical Encounter Church in Detroit, Michigan. Their growing, cross-cultural congregation, recognizes that she walks the walk that's written of and encouraged here.

The Shaunee Brannan I know, really cares about people. She invests her time in relationships and prayer. She is a leader by example. Some people have the unique ability to disarm others through appropriate humor. If you have visited the website *prayersandpunclines.com,* or if you follow Shaunee on social media, you know that her humor is loaded with healing and love. Whether it is about parenting (she and Pastor Gayle have two sweet little daughters), people at the gym, the grocery store, or rude drivers, Shaunee moves in like a stealth bomber, dropping her payload of humor and insight.

You will find some of this humor in her stories, as you turn the pages of this book. Make no mistake about it, her real intent is to help us tell ourselves the truth so God can help us heal from the crippling effects of insecurity and fear.

Rejection, abuse, victimization, divorce, unemployment, condemnation, and vicious sibling rivalry, are just a few things that start the engine of insecurity. Once started, this armored tank filled with uncertainty and fear, will steamroll your soul and leave you exhausted from the toll that life has demanded from you.

That is why we all need this book. If you read it with an open heart, the Holy Spirit will enlighten and empower you. Through the wisdom that Shaunee Brannan has lived and now describes, you too can say goodbye to insecurity.

Bishop R. Kenneth Shelton
Brighton, Michigan
February 2017

INTRODUCTION – *HI THERE*

I have very vivid memories of being a little girl, some of which I remember as if they occurred yesterday. I can smell the air, see the shade of blue that hovered in the sky that day, the aroma that lingered in the trees after it had rained the night before—30 plus years later and it's all still fresh. I look in 7th grade Cara's eyes and see fear, as she and I are pressured by the crowd of chanting classmates to escalate a verbal argument to a physical one. She was talking a good game, but her eyes were begging me to walk away. Neither of us had ever had a "real" fight. She was terrified; I was anxious to prove something to everyone.

I remember, while skipping 6th hour to get a slice of pizza, and after walking in puddles, my damp footprints outlining the pavement of downtown Detroit, where I attended Cass Technical High School. The smell of bus fumes meandered in the air, as the sound of the *Detroit People Mover* train line clacked loudly overhead, making its way through the city center. I envision the single bun on top of my head, my black-lined lips with cherry lip gloss that I sported with Guess Jeans, and a really snappy attitude. I was cute. And I knew it.

Memories of my twenties elicit fun, traveling, laughing—lots of mindless laughing, how I could cup my waist with only my thumb and forefinger, and it fit. Working out was optional, and my skin was flawless with little to no maintenance. My mind easily rehearses the faces of gentleman callers, being flattered, pursued, and how good it felt to have options. I can feel the plush seats, the strange feeling of getting into a different car to go on a date, and being overwhelmed by freshly sprayed cologne.

"Did you eat a sandwich?" I recall the confusion and innocence in my voice as I ask a young man this, on the fourth of our five dates. You see, his breath always smelled like Miracle Whip with no sandwich in sight. To this day, I don't know if it was the result of a secret food fetish, or a gland issue, but the smell was consistent; whether we met for breakfast, lunch, or dinner, it was there. Miracle Whip….as if he'd been spooning it up like yogurt. I also remember being quite petty. My pettiness made it impossible to smell Miracle Whip without explanation. Our fifth date was the last.

My thirties. My goodness. I see the fall-colored flower pedals on the runner at my wedding, the soft touch of my firstborn daughter's hand for the first time, and the tears running down my face and neck, and settling right between the "K" and "E" on my gray and pink Nike shirt, while I cried for absolutely no reason, three weeks postpartum. I see myself, five months pregnant with my second child, my forehead nestled into my pillow, and my tears igniting the smell of dormant fabric softener, as I pray to God for direction and guidance after losing my job of 13 years. The severance papers are lying there on the bed, black and white with red highlights and yellow marker by the signature line; its edges are tattered from me gripping them with a hard hand.

My mind can trace quite a few memories, seasons, events, and occasions, with vivid details. They are memories that have been imprinted on my life in some way.
They help me identify with where someone once was, where someone currently is, and where another is going.
And with what I know now, and my experiences, no matter the season, age, or time in my life, I am also able to trace the presence of INSECURITY.

It was something that had to be addressed on some level, whether through myself, or another individual. It has consistently been a part of life and growth, which required confrontation. I see this now. But I could not see it for what it was then.

It's highly likely that it may be a struggle for you as well. Very few people operate out of insecurity with the consciousness in the moment that it is, in fact, insecurity they are entertaining. It is rarely on purpose, but often innate.

Depending on what point in our lives it found root, until it is uncovered and given the exposure and label it deserves, it operates as a natural part of us, the same way that many other parts of our personality do. You can be funny, smart, spiritual, witty, and insecure, all at once. But I'd like to be a part of your process of discovery. Maybe you are that person reading this who says, "I don't need any discovery. I already know it's here." You've already recognized its presence, and how it's affected your everyday life.

Maybe you're the person reading this to diagnose someone else. You're sitting thinking: *Yeah.... 'so-n-so' could sure use this book!* You're reading this to figure out why they're so crazy and annoying, but mostly to be able to tell them that you now have hard, cold facts

xiv

via literature, that they need clinical help. You cannot wait to give them a gander at a few of these quotes! If that's you, your motive may be a little crooked, but I promise by the time you're done reading, you'll have all the backing you need for them, and a little for yourself.

No matter your reason or motive for making the decision to indulge in this book, in order for us to reach the necessary places, permission and access are required. This will be a partnership—the three of us: you, me, and God. We three are reading this together; we are laughing together, crying together, fighting together, resting together. Every emotion, every bit of resolve, every challenge, we are in it together.

So let's get some agreements on the table:

You know how you may be sick, aching, or having ailments that are outside of the natural function of your body?
So, you go to the doctor. They examine you, diagnose your condition, recommend treatment and sometimes surgery.
You are given a specific diet, limitations of activity, and overall instructions on functionality while prepping for surgery and while recovering.
None of it is fun.
None of it feels natural.
But it's fixing your sickness.
And the only thing you really have to look forward to, is that the ailment which caused the need for treatment, will finally be cured through surgery.
You can look forward to progress, change, and being whole.
But it's still not fun while going through it.

That's sort of what this will be like; there will be moments of discomfort.
For many, this will be the "aha" moment—the first time your insecurity and coping mechanisms are laid bare. This will also be the first time that, in seeing your own insecurities, you have to acknowledge that they aren't much different than everyone else's you've noticed AND pointed out.
This may make you feel naked, exposed, and vulnerable. GOOD.
There will be moments where you want to laugh with me and hug me,

then seconds later, imagine yourself slapping me. You may altogether decide that you just don't like me, and want to toss this book in the fireplace. GOOD.

In one breath, you will laugh—oh, you will snicker and be tickled. But you might get up to move after a good laugh, and realize you've been cut. And it may draw a little blood. But most medical procedures cause just a little bit of bleeding, don't they? GOOD.

You may put the book down for a day, or days, or weeks, or months (Okay. That's going too far! Don't do that, please.), before you pick it back up. GOOD.

You may try to convince yourself that insecurity isn't an issue for you, and nurse the thought: *This is a nice book.... let me see who I can give it away to.* You will probably come up with a quick list of several people who can use this book other than you. NOT GOOD.

Because for the first time, you may feel like something is wrong with you. GOOD.

You will actually begin to feel the weight of change. GOOD.

It may seem like too much at first. GOOD.

And you probably will not like it. GOOD.

Because it will include work. And for the first time, you're actually seeing that, too. GOOD.

Work we've never done before is intimidating to our established way of living and thinking.

It challenges it. It confronts it. It makes us want to fight. GOOD.

But you have to pick the right fight. You have to know where the fight should be targeted.

I am not the enemy. God is not the enemy. You are not the enemy. The enemy is insecurity and how much of a place it's found in our lives.

And even more, how comfortable we are with it there.

If it's been there for as long as mine was, it is cozy, hiding, doesn't like exposure, and will not want to leave.

No matter how tough this gets for you to face, and fail at, occasionally, do not run.

Please don't doubt your spirit's ability to fight to change. Your soul is the emotional part, it will try to rule you, and tell you that *you're just fine*, and in short, to *just give up*. But don't.

Not for one minute.

Insecurity is such an underestimated characteristic of human living. It is very subtle for some, while extremely overt for others. Its power and strength are developed through a lack of diagnosis and admission of its presence. Some don't see it, while others are ever-aware of its presence, because of the torment and anxiety it causes in everyday life. It is a silent killer of vision, a hindrance to the pursuit of dreams, and a destroyer of opportunities and relationships. It is the voice that speaks when it's not spoken to. It's the first to answer questions, and always has the last word. It looks at truth, and erases it with *one* lie. It chooses for you, and very poorly at that. It needs constant supplementing to survive, as it causes deficiency in its host, and unrest until it's quieted. It is fueled by self-doubt and fear. It looks for rejection, and usually causes you to reject yourself before anyone else can. Its roots are typically deep, and have been planted from childhood. It can only be trusted and depended on to be what it is—a taker, and never a giver. It is not gender, age, or culture based. It's an equal opportunity employer. It is not something you outgrow. It is only something you can out know.

Your knowledge will be your power; it will be your freedom.

If you cannot see it, you will never confront it.

And anything that we fail to confront, we have also failed to change.

Your 100% commitment to this is crucial. The level of commitment you have, will determine the outcome you receive. This is a part of life, no matter the venture. In addition to reading, I am asking that you participate in the *Journal Moments* included throughout the book. Journal Moments are designed to help you identify and release things that may be inside. The insight you receive about yourself will be dependent on your ability to self-evaluate. Journal Moments can be recorded several ways: you can do an audio journal, where you record your responses by voice on your phone or tablet, you can purchase a separate note pad or journal to record them in, or they can be recorded by text or memo on your phone. Whichever method you choose, make sure it is a method you can save and reflect on as you progress. Journaling our life experiences is a healthy and beneficial way to grow as individuals. It helps to add tangible commitment to a process of change. It is also a wonderful way to go back later and see thoughts and confessions that are either the same, or have changed.

The "you" that is not ruled by insecurity is a completely different person, one you need to meet. You will like *that* you. You will like *that* you A LOT. *That* you is contagious, joyful, light-hearted, reflective, wise, courageous, and in touch with themselves and others. *That* you is bursting with possibilities, as you never stop growing and blossoming into someone you never knew existed, but have always been.

By the end of the book, you will be on the path to meet *that* you. As years of hindrances fall away, much of how you've thought, planned, and pursued life, will take a new route.

I lived plagued by insecurity for years.
It shaped me in areas that ruled my life.
I made extremely poor and life-altering decisions, because of its presence.
Every bad decision I ever made, can be traced back to insecurity.
I do not want this for you.
It's not too late to change.
It's not too hard to change. It's hard. But *not* hard enough to not do it.
It's harder to stay the way you are.
Whether mildly or severely plagued by insecurity, IT MUST GO!
It's no longer welcomed.
Let's go find the places where it's lived in our lives.
And once we do, we will say, "Hi Insecurity…. Bye Insecurity," all in one breath.

Table of Contents

1

WHAT IS INSECURITY?

"Insecurity is a form of self-sabotage. If you want to fly, you have to first see your wings." - Unknown

Insecurity can be defined in many ways. Consider the dictionary.com and Merriam-Webster definitions:

INSECURITY
  1.) lack of confidence or assurance; self-doubt
  2.) the quality or state of being insecure

INSECURE
  1.) subject to fears, doubts, etc.; not self-confident or assured
  2.) not confident or certain; uneasy; anxious
  3.) not secure; exposed or liable to risk, loss, or danger
  4.) not firmly or reliably placed or fastened

SECURE
  1.) free from fear or distrust
  2.) ease of mind
  3.) assured in opinion or expectation; having no doubt
  4.) free from danger, risk, or loss; safety

These definitions describe feelings and thought patterns of individuals, which characterize them as insecure. You can also take a more personal approach and consider the wide variety of emotions insecurity has presented in your life, or in the lives of those you have interacted with. No matter how you describe your experiences with insecurity, at some point, the presence of fear will be described or mentioned. Our insecurities and fears flow from one source: our beliefs.

Our belief system is very vital and critical to our internal make-up. If you can direct a person's beliefs, you can direct that person. What we believe, anchors us, directs our actions, and dictates what we deem valuable. The things we believe to be true or false are the things we live by— things that alter our decision-making and affect our lives.

As a result, what we believe about God, determines what we believe about ourselves. What we believe about both God and ourselves, determines what we think about others, how we view life, and our level of security and insecurity.

We live by what we believe both consciously and subconsciously, even when what we believe is false. Something that is very much false, or a lie, is only successful when it finds place to be accepted as truth. What may be false to one person, may be true to another. You can see this in all the different religions people adopt as paths of spirituality. Buddhists, Catholics, Baptists, Pentecostals, Atheists, New Age, Lutheran, Seventh Day Adventists, and all such others, believe they have all found the one truth in regard to spirituality. In looking at this list and considering the many others I did not mention, it's safe to say that SOMEONE is wrong. It is unlikely to have this many options, and everyone be right in all points of their spiritual path. Those who have it wrong and are, in fact, following a spiritual belief system that is false, still perceive their system as true. Truth to us that really is not truth at all, is still truth to us, because what we believe to be true, is where we find security in our decision-making.

Let me further state that unbelief is still a form of belief. Not believing in a thing is only the result of what you have chosen to believe. Belief is the result of our truth. Once we have decided what we believe, then and only then, can we decide what we don't believe. We stand firm on what we believe to be false by the truth that anchors us. We live by what is true first, and what we believe to be false is a secondary confirmation. Even an Atheist's spiritual path is founded in belief. They believe that God does not exist. As a result, their resolve and decisions do not include the possibility of divine intervention, help, and instruction. Instead, they have replaced their belief in God with a belief in humanity and things that are visible to the eye. They live believing only in what can be produced by themselves and others. Those who are Agnostic, profess that they do not know what is true concerning God and His existence. They are not convinced that He does or does not exist. They are often confused with Atheists or labeled as such since, from the point-of-view of those who only believe in absolutes, for a person to say they "don't know" if God exists, is to say they don't believe in God at all. But even the Agnostic has an adopted belief. The difference is that what they believe

2

fluctuates according to information they grasp in a moment or season. But it is an unstable truth that has not yet been confirmed to them. As a result, they make no claim to commit to a specific truth but, instead, remain open to possibilities. Their current level of truth, or what they have identified with, can be seen in how they are currently living, though it is always subject to change.

Whether or not we believe in God, it is impossible for a human being not to believe something. Our conscience, mental construct, and brain, are each built to attach to truth. Our senses serve the purpose of providing truth to us. Using sight, sound, touch, taste, and smell, we learn and confirm all of the outputs of life. They assist our brains in the process of gathering information. Only a person who doesn't have all these things, is left without tools to gather information for their beliefs. In spite of them living, they are in a vegetative state. There is no way around being human and not believing. To know who you are, I want to know what you believe, not what you don't believe. If you can tell me what you believe, I already know what you don't believe.

You can live out a lie and reap all of its damage, but still not understand that it's false until it contradicts itself. Most things are not seen as false until what they promise falls short. This is often when we are willing to open up to the possibility that we've missed something very vital in gaining truth. This does not just apply to religion, but all things in our lives. What we believe as truth, is our truth, false or not, if it's found place in our belief system as viable—it is part of the source we pull from for direction.

It is very difficult to describe our securities or insecurities without, at some point, referencing fear. For many, the presence of insecurity, or the lack thereof, simply boils down to what they do or do not fear. What is feared may vary from person to person, but ultimately, there is fear of exposure to danger, criticism, and rejection, which results from our beliefs about God that produce our sense of self-worth and ability.

In essence, our insecurities are the sum of our mental resolves and beliefs. Based on what we believe, we determine what is stable or unstable. Insecurity is the emotional feeling that accompanies the evaluation of a thing as not being sure, stable, or safe. These things typically call for our interaction, involvement, commitment, or trust. When we resolve that something is not sure, true, stable, or safe, we often feel apprehensive about it and have a lack of trust in it. Being forced to go around these feelings typically results in the emergence of

3

fear.

As a matter of fact, all of our emotions and feelings, not just insecurity, are rooted in our belief system. Your passions, what makes you angry, what makes you feel strife, what makes you laugh, or feel happy, are all reflections of what you believe. I have heard insecurity summarized as a fear, while others suggest it is the *result* of what we fear. But the question of whether or not insecurity is a form of fear, does not fall into a black or white category—it cannot be easily answered.

It's possible to sense danger, but not feel fear. Whether or not a person feels fear is dependent on what they believe to be the possible outcome of their perceived danger and how it affects them. Again, this determining factor points to what we believe. You'll find that the presence of one emotion makes way for another, just as one belief creates or strengthens another. It is a mental chain in our make-up that revolves and, when traced, points back to one place—what we believe. By dealing with what you believe, we are able to deal with why you are insecure.

THE FEAR FACTOR

"I have self-doubt. I have insecurity. I have fear of failure. I have nights when I show up at the arena and I'm like, 'My back hurts, my feet hurt, my knees hurt. I don't have it. I just want to chill.' We all have self-doubt. You don't deny it, but you also don't capitulate to it. You embrace it."
- Kobe Bryant

While we continue learning about insecurity, "The Fear Factor" will be a resounding theme. As I mentioned before, I am careful not to give a black and white or "yes" or "no" answer to the question of whether or not insecurity is simply a fear. Doing so could cause you to form conclusions that prevent you from seeing all that lies in between in the gray areas.

Feelings of fear and anxiety work hand-in-hand with insecurity. They accompany insecurity and make it effective. They are often what makes it uncomfortable and evident. Without them, we would not know how to label insecurity or recognize its unnatural functionality in us. Fear brings finality to moments of insecurity—it's the result we wish against. It influences our beliefs regarding the possible outcomes

4

of triggered insecurity, whether momentarily or habitually.

Where fear has found a foothold, it is impossible to eliminate insecurity. Fear strengthens the presence of insecurity because it fuels it. It convinces us that our insecurities are legitimate, even when they are not. It's possible to fear something that actually has no level of danger or harm, because our insecurity has convinced us that it's, indeed, dangerous and harmful. For example, take the woman who climbs a chair and screams for dear life when she sees a spider on the floor. How about the man who stands in front of a crowd, stuttering and stammering with sweaty palms because he's plagued with stage fright? There is also the person who, due to his or her fear of heights, faints on an elevator after its climbed to a high floor.

These responses would not occur without fear preceding the events. In reality, the spiders we see are typically able to be contained without us being bitten. Standing in front of a crowd to speak, poses no threat to our lives. The average elevator ride is 10 seconds, and is not typically hazardous. However, in the moment, it would take careful rationalizing to modify the responses of people who perceive that they are in harmful situations.

Our insecurities, in the unhealthiest instances, are the sum of our fears. I pluralize fear because it is possible to fear in one area, but not another. It's possible to be afraid of three specific things, and free from fear regarding other things. Some people have one great fear, and thus, one great insecurity. It is highly possible to trust God's ability in one area, but not in another. The area where fear resides, is also the area of our insecurity. If you nip your fear, you will nip your insecurity.

Again, going back to our thought life, we recognize that what we believe about God and ourselves produces fear, it also produces our sense of love for and by others. Just as we can look at our level of fear and see a reflection of our insecurities, we can look at our perception and level of love and see our security. It is the cause and effect—the Yin to our Yang. There is no way around it.

Journal Moment

What are you afraid of? What do you classify as your fears?

Everyone has their own mental classifications of their strengths, weaknesses, limitations, and perceived inadequacies. Think of the strongest and most confident person you know. THEY HAVE THEM TOO. Not being transparent or not discussing them should never be used to indicate whether or not insecurities exist. People are usually uncomfortable mentioning their insecurities and/or fears, as these are very personal parts of our lives that point to who we truly are, beyond what is seen. Some feel that mentioning their insecurities will draw negative attention to them or cause them to be viewed in a way opposite of their preference. Others are either working hard to get rid of them, or are still in denial regarding their insecurities.

THE BREAKDOWN

By considering insecurity, along with how it evolves and operates in our lives over time, I have divided it into two types, so that we might take a step closer to understanding it. Contrary to popular belief, not all insecurity should be described as unhealthy. There is a form of insecurity that is a natural response to the unknown and untested, driven by uncertainty. It is part of the human ability to evaluate and assess. Without a healthy form of insecurity at different times in our lives, we would not value or take advantage of the ability to overcome obstacles and fear, to discover untapped potential, or recognize and appreciate differences in one another. We will further discuss what this healthy insecurity, also referred to as *Circumstantial insecurity*, looks like. However, the type of insecurity that we will deal with in length, and bid farewell, is *Characteristic insecurity*. It is the unhealthiest and most debilitating form of insecurity that people bear, preventing individuality, the ability to trust, and progressiveness. This type of insecurity IS actually rooted in fear, whether minimally, or abundantly—fear produces it.

Feelings of insecurity surface with the presentation of an opportunity, or an occasion that calls for qualities or authority that you are either not sure you are capable of producing, or sure that you cannot produce, whether because of lack, or uncertainty of self. It is the fear that what you have resolved as your shortcomings or inadequacies may be seen by others. It is fear of failure and exposure. It is the presence of anxiety and worry in advance, with or without reason. We often view insecurity in terms of how we live and interact with others, but it must first be viewed in terms of how we interact with ourselves. In other words, insecurity, in some way, shape, or form, is the foundational thought: *I am not good enough.* It is the thought that eliminates you as a contender for whichever opportunity is presented. It can further be customized to each individual's belief, in addition to methods of coping with and satisfying insecurity.

"I am not good enough to _____."
"I am not good enough without _____."
"I am not good enough for _____."

So on, and so forth.

The options to fill in the blanks are vast, since the same is true of life's endless list of opportunities. When we feel the presence of insecurity, we have consciously or unconsciously filled in the blank.

Journal Moment

Consider goals you have made, challenges you have accepted, opportunities that have presented themselves, and how you have responded. Please write your thoughts about failing to complete your goals, follow through with challenges, or to accept opportunities. Be mindful of how this made you feel. Fill in the blank with accompanying words if the thought "I am not good enough _____" crossed your mind during that time. Write every thought you can remember.

TRANSPARENCY MOMENT: BEING IN DENIAL

Once upon a time, insecurity was a four-letter word for me: WEAK. I hated it. I hated to be labeled insecure. I hated to be viewed as insecure, even if it was my reality. I considered it a major weakness; I interpreted it as vulnerability. I wanted to appear strong, put together, and sure of myself, even if I was not. I remember several speeches from my father regarding what a "weak" woman looked like. It was his effort to keep my sister and me away from "no-good men," as he put it. He'd tell us several stories of mistakes he'd watched his mother and sisters make. He'd hoped to raise strong, self-confident women.

"Shaunee, be a leader and not a follower!" He often reminded me. I'd heard this my whole life. It was ingrained in me that I had two options: "To lead, or to follow," and following was the undesirable option. To me, some of the worst things a person could ever be, were needy and insecure.

Growing up in competitive settings was also a considerable factor. In both church and school, peer pressure was predominant. Teasing and being teased were prevalent when dealing with other children. I also found it to be just as prevalent as an adult. In my truest form, I was innocent, kind-hearted, trusting, prone to feel compassion at the drop of a hat, and full of laughter. But in many of the settings I was in, I soon learned these qualities were exploited. After being manipulated, taken advantage of, and betrayed one too many times by people who I'd trusted to be something entirely different, I decided I didn't like the way it felt. I also decided not to allow it to happen to me again. I promised myself that I had to somehow toughen up, smarten up, and be a step ahead. My desire to toughen up and look out more for myself, was my effort to never feel such helplessness and WEAKNESS again.

I'd gotten pretty far in life masking my insecurities. I think I mostly owed the success of this accomplishment to my being in the dark about what my issues really were. It wasn't a matter of me being in denial, I was flat out blind. I didn't see it. The reality is, you can lie to yourself for so long, be labeled as something else, and utilize coping mechanisms, to the point that your lies become truth to you, and your problems become buried beneath a false surface. This also contributes to you being able to convince others. For those of you who are reading this book with the realization that insecurity is a struggle for you, congratulations! You're already a step ahead of a lot of people. Before a person can be freed from this debilitating mindset, they often have to be convinced that it's there.

My blindness did not consist of the thought that I had never been insecure. I was aware that it was something I'd began feeling from a very young age; however, with time, opportunities, and growth, I believed it was something I'd whipped once and for all, and that it was no longer present. Accomplishments, people, possessions, and God, yes God, were all things I unconsciously misused, which enabled my blindness. My theology concerning God and life, were, at times, a large part of my incorrect view in this area. I did not understand progressive freedom, nor constant dependability on God for my thorns. I was under the notion that I was cured; I was to ask no questions about how it happened, nor about any lingering symptoms. To think anything other than that, brought into question who I believed God was, and what He was capable of. I was not ready to ask that question, so, I learned to suppress anything that was contrary to what I had already been "freed" from.

It wasn't until I'd met my husband, that the light bulb began to flicker again. We were still in the dating stage, and he and I were having a disagreement. I'd just gotten done reciting to him a list of recommendations and thoughts concerning what he could work on and it was all true; however, by the time I was done, he sat there staring at me with naked eyes. This was a man who was not used to someone reading his mail, but in my natural ability, I'd read it from the rooty to the tooty. He was amazed at what I could see—beyond his gifts, talents, and him being celebrated in most circles. I was the one voice pushing for change in the areas that needed work. Furthermore, I was not afraid to say what needed to be said. He squirmed, glared, and put up a little fight, but eventually, he listened. I felt so good about myself. I remember a great feeling of satisfaction. I knew I was spot on. It hadn't dawned on me that with the same access I had to deliver a message, it was also meant for me to receive one.

Shortly thereafter, we attended an industry event together. This was my first time bringing him into my world. I remember carefully picking out my attire, taking my time with my hair and makeup, and inquiring as to what he was wearing. He was coming with me, and I wanted him to look good. We had to look the part, like we belonged together. We enjoyed the evening, or so I thought. We got in the car and proceeded to my house.

"Shaunee, you changed in there," he said while we were driving.

"What do you mean?!" I asked.

"I don't know, you just weren't the same," he answered. I was baffled and I started to feel defensive.

"Like how? Like…. give me examples!"

He went on to describe different instances, noting several details that, quite frankly, I was stunned to find out he caught. He went down his mental list of things he'd cataloged, and as he went on, I could feel heat rising from my toes to my scalp. The more he talked, I thought: *Well my God, this man can't even remember people's names, birthdays, dates, events, nothing, yet he's not at a loss for details right now!* In short, he described a person I really hated. He described someone self-centered, snobby, phony, and both extrovert and introvert at the wrong times. So as I refuted every example he offered, occasionally calling him a liar, he remained patient, and almost slightly smug. He knew he was right, and even more, he knew he was pushing my buttons—the ones that were never pushed and never exposed—the ones I'd pushed in him just a few weeks before. Just when I thought he was done, he said:

"Shaunee, you struggle with insecurity. That's the reason." I don't know what he said after that because his voice morphed into Charlie Brown's teacher. I'd rather he had called me anything, *anything at all* besides insecure. I began feeling light-headed and nauseous as I started having a slight out-of-body experience. I envisioned us in one of those really dramatic soap opera scenes, one that included me slapping him right there on the spot— slapping the living daylight out of him, hard enough to give him whiplash. I was that upset. I think my jaw dropped to my toes. My mouth had to be open for a while, because by the time I found the breath and mental capacity to speak, I had to take several gulps to re-moisten my vocal chords.

"Who's insecure?!" Out came a squeak at least five octaves higher than my natural voice. My neck was contorted, my posture tense, my bottom lip quivered like I'd been electrocuted. I could feel my face tingling resulting from the alarm set off in my nervous system. *Shaunee…. after he drops you off, dump him, and slam his car door for added emphasis.* This was the first thought that came to my mind.

10

His words instantaneously turned me into the Tasmanian Devil. I went on a rant. I denied his claims. I even diverted back to the conversation we'd had a few weeks before about his issues, reiterating that they were still there and needed his attention. I took each instance he'd given, and carefully dismantled it. I argued it was all his imagination, or *HIS* insecurities, and once I was done, I didn't feel any better. To say I was mad is like calling the Atlantic Ocean a pond. I was boiling. Burnt. Sizzled to a crisp. Incensed. I felt exposed, vulnerable, and naked. My defense mechanisms went into overdrive. At the end of the day, I'm a realist, and, whether I liked it or not, he was equally as good as I was at "seeing" people, and he'd seen me. I was very afraid that everything he'd said was true; it felt like a dead ringer. His diagnosis had found a match with my actions, and I was panicking. I'd worked hard to build this shell, and it felt like he was tapping into all the uncomfortable places inside me.

He didn't know it, but when I got home, I sat on the edge of my bed and replayed the entire evening all the way down to me walking into the house. I got up, walked over to my dresser mirror, and gazed at my reflection. I looked at the details of my carefully done makeup, flawless attire, and hair that was the perfect product of 8 hours of sleeping on hard rollers. I put on my pajamas, cut the lights off, got in the bed, laid my head on my pillow, and cried. I cried like a baby— like a hungry baby. It was the first time I thought to myself: *Oh no... it's back*. The truth was, it had never really left. Its roots were deep, and God was exposing its fruit to gain access to its roots. Where He was taking me and the plans He had for my life, did not include the presence of insecurity. They did not include a lack of identity. There was no way around it. He was not going to let me continue this way. It was time for me to deal with it for real.

I believe it's your time, too. Perhaps you've reached the point in your life where you no longer want to run from changing what has always seemed so hard. Maybe this will be the first time you truly see your areas of insecurity and how they have affected you, perhaps your entire life. Or, maybe being in denial is a defense mechanism that has provided you the escape you find comfort in without having to challenge yourself. If you have set out to reach goals, to fulfill potential, to grasp destiny, or simply make it through the day without feeling inadequate, IT'S POSSIBLE. It is not a far-fetched dream. It is not a fantasy or desire that cannot be obtained. In case no one has ever told you and you've never told yourself, YOU CAN CHANGE. This is not too hard. It's harder to stay in a state of self-destruction, knowingly or unknowingly.

This is not just another book. This is not just another way to past time. This is an opportunity for you to grasp your new season, transition, and fulfillment, and to hold it tight. THIS time is not like all the others. THIS time it will not get away. THIS time you will continue into change. THIS time you will not give up or abort the process because of laziness, discomfort, complacency, or fear. THIS time you will see what needs to be seen. And as truth floods your soul and spirit, you will be set free.

LET'S GO!

2

CIRCUMSTANTIAL INSECURITY

"It is an old adage, that the way to be safe is to never be secure. Each one of us requires the spur of insecurity to force us to do our best."
- Harold W. Dodds

As I stated before, I don't prefer a black or white answer regarding what insecurity really is. As one who has dealt with it in several of its stages, ranging from mild to extreme, I feel if I were to force it into a simple answer, I'd be cheating myself out of the benefit of really good experiences and bragging rights that came from carrying the plague of insecurity, and finally, kicking its butt. To see it for what it truly is and to be able to uncover it in your own life, is magical. You almost instantly start to get answers. One answered question, leads to another that is answered. I dare not rob you of the chance to get there a lot faster than I did. So I'll elaborate as much as possible to help close the gap of unknowns for you.

There are many things that create joy and excitement in life. Though we often complain about it and surely run from it, the gift of *challenge* is a vital part of life. Without challenges, we would not have much to hope for. We typically don't hope for things that are easy to obtain or readily accessible. Things that are challenging usually require work, effort, resources, and dedication. When we overcome challenges, they become accomplishments we hold dear. This is where circumstantial insecurity surfaces.

Insecurity that operates on a circumstantial basis is specific to the occasion. It is the feeling of not being secure when we are a direct or indirect candidate to fulfill a duty, role, expectation, or need, for which we feel ill-equipped, do not possess the skill set, or lack interest. Circumstantial insecurity is typically found in the moment an opportunity is presented, and in us contemplating our acceptance or decline of it. In essence, it is the evaluation period before you arrive to a "yes" or "no."

All individuals, regardless of their strengths, weaknesses, race, culture, gender, age, riches or poverty, and so forth, are faced with circumstantial insecurity. It has become a common belief that people who are self-confident have a good amount of self-esteem, and those who do not have poor opinions of themselves, are not faced with insecurity. As I expound on this type of insecurity, you will gain the understanding that circumstantial insecurity is not an attribute of a person, but an attribute of life. It is not a characteristic of your identity, but event-induced and a characteristic of life. It is often the natural response to the unknown. Experiencing this type of insecurity is not a sign of weakness, but a sign of being human. However, the way it is processed and confronted is a tell-tale sign of your internal structure. When it is processed in an unhealthy way, it is a sign of *Characteristic insecurity,* which we will deal with in the next chapter. In order to possess the quality and ability to process circumstantial insecurity appropriately, is a strength and something to be admired.

THE BREAKDOWN

Let me give you a few examples to help broaden your understanding:

If someone were to ask me to perform a vocal solo, I would be able to do it without a second thought. Singing is something I have done since I was very young. I am both familiar and comfortable with the strengths and weaknesses of my vocal ability. I am sure of my ability to produce a quality product that has the potential to be enjoyable in this area; however, if someone were to ask me to perform a dance selection, this would elicit feelings opposite of the comfort I feel while singing. I dance for recreation, and for fun. The fun of it is that no one is watching, critiquing, or expecting to be entertained while I dance. There is no pressure for me to live up to an expectation of some sort; I do not feel pressure to deliver a desired result to anyone. The thought of dancing to entertain others, makes me take into consideration what I believe concerning my dancing abilities, which are limited. Unlike singing, I was not born with an advanced natural ability or talent to dance. I have never received technical training of any kind, nor do I have lengthy experience in dancing. In all honesty, I have never nursed a great desire to dance as a professional, nor have I hoped to be a good dancer to the point that I'd considered investing in it. I have never sat back and said to myself, "Boy, I wish I could dance!" Nope—not ever. My dancing ability is good enough for what I like to use it for. My current abilities have served me well enough.

The idea of dancing WITH others produces feelings of joy and fun. The thought of professionally dancing FOR others, makes me feel insecure in regard to what I may produce in comparison to what is expected. I am very comfortable saying that considering all genres of dance, I am not a professional, nor do I want to be. Could I be taught and trained? Based on what I've accomplished without training, with only my natural ability, I believe so. Yet, I am self-aware enough to assess that this is not an interest I desire to give time or attention to.

Continue lending me your imagination.

Imagine being on a flight. The flight attendant comes down the aisle and you notice her rush to the side of one of the passengers sitting directly across from you. She frantically screams, "Is there a doctor on board?! He's not breathing! We need a doctor!" There is no response from any of the passengers. She hurriedly turns to you, and says, "You! Can you help me? Do you know CPR?"

Think about the immediate thoughts and feelings that come to your mind. If you are like me, you do not know CPR. Sure, you've watched a few episodes of *ER* on Tuesday nights, but you know that doesn't count as certified training. I am a fairly secure, self-aware individual, and I'm telling you right here and now, I would probably need an adult diaper. I can imagine my tongue stammering and my face getting hot. I can feel my head shaking back and forth, "NO!" while writing this. Every second they are waiting, depending on me, his life is fading into the distance, and if I dare even flub my way through it, he'd have so much slobber on his face from my attempt at mouth-to-mouth resuscitation, and a smashed nose from me pinching it. I wouldn't even attempt it. I'd seek someone skilled, and I would not feel bad about passing up on what could possibly be a major victory. My assessment of the moment, opportunity, time allotted, risk(s) associated, and my ability, are all factors to be considered.

On the other hand, let's imagine no doctor came forward. Let's imagine no one who knew CPR came forward, as a matter of fact, no one came forward at all. And as time passed, I sat there watching him lose consciousness. Even in my inexperience and lack of education, there is a side to me that believes enough in hidden ability to try. YES, with no other option, I would try. With no training, there is a high possibility I could fail to provide adequate CPR and revive him, but my desire to see him live outweighs my belief concerning my ability to save him. I would do the best I could. The greater good would cause me to press beyond my evaluation of my ability, with the hope of saving his life.

Circumstantial insecurity is both natural and normal. All human beings experience this throughout life. How we process circumstantial insecurity is determined by our security level within ourselves, and our ability to make logical assessments. It requires a comfortable level of knowledge concerning our strengths, weaknesses, skill level, and interests. The basis of what we believe helps us not to view something we are unable to do as a finality to who we are, or as the sum of our value altogether. We are also able to assess our willingness to grow in that area if necessary, and decide whether or not it's an interest worth pursuing. Logical processing also takes into consideration the time and resources needed for this pursuit, and if after time and thought, the answer is still, "I cannot do this," it is not viewed as a weakness, but the result of one's strength to understand where their talent and ability is best suited.

Circumstantial insecurity is sometimes the entry point by which we take on new ventures and interests. Wondering about our ability is sometimes the thing that causes us to find out how much of it we already have or are capable of having. It is the side of us that evaluates the challenge and says, "I believe I can." Everyone is born with a certain amount of natural ability. Then there is the ability that we develop from scratch, meaning it was both created and cultivated by our interest and practice. But no matter its origin, the extent of all ability is realized when it is cultivated. The strength and potency of our ability is seen with exposure, time, commitment, practice, and the chance to meet the need the ability is called to meet.

Journal Moment

Think of a time you were faced with circumstantial insecurity. How did you respond to it? To this day, do you think it was the appropriate response? Try to think of moments in which you believe you gave the right response and wrong response to circumstantial insecurity. Be sure to write down your feelings concerning them, including the presence of any regrets or satisfaction.

CIRCUMSTANTAL INSECURITY & THE CONTROL FREAK

"As kryptonite was to Superman, thus is the unknown to a Control Freak." - Shaunee Brannan

Circumstantial insecurity can be difficult for some individuals to process. Those who struggle with characteristic insecurity especially find it hard because they carry the presence of insecurity with them as a part of their character. It is not something that comes or goes with the moment, it's there. As a result, they filter most of life's events through insecurity, even moments that are circumstantial or temporary.

It can also be difficult for control freaks and habitually organized individuals. As one who has the tendency to be very controlled and planned, I can tell you we get a lot of credit for being "put together." People marvel at our planning abilities and thorough thought processes. The truth is, some of it is talent and perfected quality, while other parts are the results of hazard prevention. Most control freaks struggle with fear. The idea is that the more control they have, the greater opportunity they have to prevent calamity, and without calamity, they do not have to fear.

When going through transitional periods in our lives and experiencing new seasons, these are often the times when circumstantial insecurities surface. During the "in-between" stage, the stage right in the middle of transitioning from one place to another, circumstantial insecurity is prevalent. At this stage nothing is settled. Nothing is sure. You are providing maintenance to where you were and where you are going all at the same time. For people who operate best with control, God uses this "in-between" stage to reveal to you how much control is yours, and how much belongs to Him. The ability that we may carry to help us in the next stage has not yet materialized. It only materializes as we trust God to take us there.

The truth of the matter is, once we say yes to God, like, REALLY say yes, the only control entrusted to us is our level of submission and our stewardship over things in our lives. That's it. He is in control of everything else. He decides much of where the car is driven. You just need to buckle your seatbelt. It is a breaking place. Any dependency on Him that we have forfeited to trust in ourselves or lean to our own understanding, is shown at this stage. It is a place where our security is not perceived in our ability, but in His. For those who trust God, the ones who trust Him FOR REAL, this is the process that we live by. But this type of decision to trust God blindly, is only possible through our perception of security. For the one who views God as a safe place, it is second nature to trust Him. But for the one who has struggled to view Him as a safe place or trustworthy, this type of trust feels like the gamble of a lifetime.

People described as control freaks, even those that are self-described, are, at their core, people working to keep their fears from materializing. They are individuals whose insecurities have graduated to a level where they are managed through extreme control. Opportunities and events produced by circumstantial insecurity are almost always responded to with a "no" by a control freak. They are uncomfortable saying "yes" for fear of loss of control. They would rather pass up on a possible positive outcome for what they already have, even if it's less than favorable, because it is familiar. In short, they do not gamble. They live in the familiar. It is their friend and safety net. Testing new waters is only done after thorough investigation of the liabilities, and even then, it's done with a life vest and a great level of anxiety. While dealing with the unknown, they wrestle with themselves and others, until they finally return back to a place of common ground.

It's possible to be a control freak in one area, but not another. No matter where you choose to execute control, it will always be the area of your greatest proclivity to fear. That is the area where a control freak grasps the greatest control. The notion is that the greater the amount of control they have in a particular area, the greater amount of control they have over an
outcome concerning that area.

A HEALTHY INSECURITY

Circumstantial insecurity, when processed correctly, is a reflection of our state of mind. I have experienced just as many proud moments saying, "No, I can't," as I have saying, "Yes, I can." Being able to say "no" left room for others who were meant to say "yes." Saying "yes" produced moments for me to thrive at the exposure of my ability, or gave reality to dormant ones. It took me some time, but eventually I learned that saying "yes" or "no" at the right time, positioned me to hear "yes" or "no" at the right time. It was not only an eye-opener, but a door-opener. People not only gravitated to this type of confidence, but respected it as well. Not many people apply critical thinking while evaluating what's being asked of them; instead, insecurity is the filter by which they make their evaluations. Those who have not yet reached a place of internal security and acceptance, often respond in whichever way gains them acceptance or makes them feel less insecure, even if they are not qualified to fill the need they've committed to. An example of this would be me, in an effort to gain acceptance, deciding to attempt a dance selection anyway, in spite of my admitted lack of ability, training, and interest. This is an example of using circumstantial insecurity in a negative way. Motive and intention are both very critical factors in evaluating the presence of insecurity. By assessing our predominant thought(s) and desired outcome, we are able to determine if we're overcoming because we know who we are, or if we're working to overcome in an effort to learn who we are. Using these moments as an attempt to add value to ourselves robs us of our true benefit, often leaving us in a state of disappointment if we fail at our endeavor.

TRANSPARENCY MOMENT: CRY BABY

Once upon a time I did not have a balanced view of my abilities and inabilities. I viewed all inability as a weakness, and leaned on my abilities as the defining factor of my worth. I would end up saying "yes" or "no" at all the wrong times. It was an anxiety filled reality and I lived in discomfort. My spirit knew it was unhealthy, but my soul (mind, will, and emotions) didn't yet know how to change much of anything.

I can remember when Haven, my first born child, came along. Shew! I laugh thinking of how prepared I thought I was in comparison to what I needed to be. Let me just start by telling you that I had about a month of postpartum depression (PPD) after having her. I'd heard people talk about it, I'd even had a close girlfriend caution me, having had it herself. But I hadn't given it a second thought. I really thought I was immune. To this day, I don't know if it were pride or ignorance, maybe a bit of both, but it was not a concern of mine. I'd read several books and online newsletters, all prepping me for breastfeeding, sleeping schedules, the perfect nursery, etc., etc. They'd all talked about PPD, but I'd either skimmed over it, or sat there reading testimonials thinking: *Those poor women. They must not know Jesus*, or that they had to be mentally unstable long before a baby came along for PPD to have been possible. *It's not the baby. You just crazy, girl!* That's what I thought. Lord—I laugh at myself now!

When going into labor, Haven's heart rate dropped suddenly and I had to have a C-section delivery. Up until this point, I did what the heck I wanted to—I'd lived a very full and free single life. I'd traveled extensively and lived on my terms and my schedule. Even after I was married, there wasn't a huge difference in that I had time to do what I wanted and needed to do. I would go from one place to the other, one commitment to the other, the gym, the mall, church, and everywhere else, with neither a schedule nor a thought for time and its scarcity. I literally worked until two days before my delivery, and was in the gym the day before I went into the hospital to be induced. I never stopped moving.

Within a week, I went from enjoying my freedom, to being home bound and in pain, recovering from being cut wide open. On top of that, I love a clean home. This is the first time I'm willing to admit publicly (knowing that my husband will eventually use this against me), but I love a clean home to the point that I'm slightly clinically insane until it's clean. I turn into a crazy person, and not being able to clean my house because of my surgery, made me feel like a dirtball. My husband would look around and say, "Shaunee, there is nothing wrong with this house! It is already clean," but our perceptions of clean are completely different. I'd made a habit of walking around the house cleaning up after him and the dog every day, but having a C-section limited my activity so I couldn't do those things anymore. Sometimes I would look at the little drops of pee that ended up on the neck of the toilet from my husband's midnight trips, (men, stop doing this to us, it makes us say bad things about you to God) and not being able to bend over and clean them up would set me off. I would cry.

I was a new mom, and didn't know how to let Haven cry like babies do. The minute she got started, I'd pick her up. I held her while I did EVERYTHING. Her crying was the worst thing in the world to me; it made me a prisoner. I could only do things if she was asleep. Sometimes I had to choose between a nap and a shower during her still moments. Most times the nap won. And until my relief came to watch her, I'd be walking around my house, holding Haven, smelling like liver and onions with dewy areas of my human anatomy. Such a beautiful shower in sight, with no chance I'd get to use it. And I would cry.

Then there was the breast feeding which was going exceptionally well for Haven. She didn't miss a feeding. Not one. She ate all day and night. ALL NIGHT. I don't think anything could have prepared me for the jolt to my reality that I would go from sleeping eight to nine hours to three. As soon as I'd get into a deep sleep, she'd be ready to eat. And I would cry.

Then there was the shock of what all this breastfeeding did to my boobs (insert laugh of insanity here).

Disclaimer
Men, non-mothers, teenagers, aliens, and all others who have never had a baby—I'm just going to say sorry in advance. Nursing mothers and women who have breastfed talk about breasts, babies, and body parts like farmers talk about cows and corn—IT'S NOTHING TO US.

So about these boobs. They went from apples to melons. Not the nice melons you're proud of and would like to have forever, the "inconvenient" type of boobs that are just in the way. I'd fall asleep and wake up with my chin wedged between them. They were REALLY disobedient and aggressive, lopsided at the wrong times, and made all of my cute little shirts look like I'd stolen some poor toddler's wardrobe. My shoulders and back broadened to support them, and I almost got picked up on the defensive line for the Detroit Lions. The first week, my nipples felt like they'd been hit by lightning, or put on a barbecue pit. They were the sorest things on my body. I'd cringe when she was ready to eat. And when she wasn't eating, I was walking around with ice packs on them. When I realized I'd have to buy all new bra's and what they would cost me, my realist side kicked in. Knowing these things would eventually deflate and turn into raisins, it seemed like a more logical decision to settle for some Saran Wrap and an arm sling for each of them to whip them up and strap them down, instead of purchasing all new bras. And if by some stroke of God's goodness, Haven overslept, the blessing of finally getting some sleep was actually a curse of "rock boobs." I'd wake up with lumpy and impacted breasts, sometimes so full that it was difficult for her to feed. And I would cry.

I think I cried about everything. It wasn't until I'd finally gotten out of the house one day and we were leaving the store, that something else set me off and I couldn't stop crying. My husband turned to me and said, "Shaunee, what is wrong with you? You are not an emotional person. You've been crying a lot lately. It's actually cute. It's not like you at all!" That's when I realized I didn't want to be cute. I wanted to stop the crying. It was becoming ridiculous. I had other things to worry about, like a newborn baby and my husband's pee drops on my toilet. I couldn't be wasting time crying. It took two weeks, but right there it dawned on me, "I wonder if this is postpartum depression," I said to myself. I called my mom and asked her if she'd had it and what it felt like. She said she had it with two of her four children and described it. I knew then that it was, in fact, PPD I was dealing with. And that's right, you guessed it—I CRIED!

The truth is, my postpartum depression was circumstantially induced. It was a new situation I was sure I could handle until it got there. Nothing prepared me for the amount of love I'd feel for such a sweet little baby and her complete and total dependency on us. For the first time in life, I was feeling the weight of the responsibility to secure life for her. I wasn't thinking in just the moment, but the next 25 years of her life, and it made me scared. I questioned our ability. I wanted so desperately to give her everything she needed, but I saw that with time and effort, I was capable. I didn't know I could be a mother until I had to be one. My interest was there, but my confidence wasn't. Eventually it came, and I saw that just like many other abilities, I had the ability, which was once dormant, to be a mom. Not just a mom, but a rock star mom.

TAKING ADVANTAGE

To those who may be coming out of, or who are in the middle of a very personal and difficult season, where circumstantial insecurity is prevalent and the unknown is at every turn, let not your hearts be troubled. Divorce, death, diagnosis, termination, and loss of any kind, can be hard to face. Comforts, and stabilities we once depended on and lived by have been removed, leaving gaps we don't quite know how to fill. Though these may be some of the most extreme forms, they are still opportunities for circumstantial insecurity to rise, and like the least extreme forms, you have it within you to navigate them. This is a beautiful opportunity to reap the benefits of things that have befallen you—things you perhaps never anticipated. You can go through your trial with misery, strife, bitterness, and anger in your heart, or you can go through it with the full intention of making it to your destination stronger, happier, wiser, and better. This circumstance is meant to pull everything out of you that is dormant. It is meant to show you who you truly are. It's ground that's fertile, waiting on you to cultivate it with your courage. Do not shy away. Do not seek the weak option. Pull on what little hope may remain—work it, feed it, multiply it. This is not just the end of something, but the beginning of something you never knew existed.

When faced with circumstantial insecurity, people who are secure in their identity view this as another emotion to process, the same as they do others such as anger, pride, frustration, sadness, joy, and many others. How we process feelings and emotions serves as a mirror, displaying how we feel about ourselves. Depending on our level of self-confidence, self-esteem, self-respect, and self-love, we make evaluations and perceptions, and act out of the understanding and mindset these things produce. A person with an unhealthy sense of self, responds to circumstantial insecurity with an imbalance. Since characteristic insecurity is usually present at some level, they absorb circumstantial insecurity as a flaw, as opposed to a part of life and a reflection of who they are as a person. A person who experiences circumstantial insecurity is not weak or inferior. Such a feeling is part of being human and growing into who we are.

If everyone were able to do all the same things and be the same type of people, we would never value our abilities, as they would be too comparable. Circumstantial insecurity is often the response to a need, desire, or opportunity, for which we are not gifted or have not invested the time or interest necessary to indulge in it. Responding to it the right way can cause the feelings to disappear as quickly as they come. Saying "yes" or "no" based on the situation and our known or unknown abilities, frees us to experience the joy and pride that come with being able deliver on things we are actually equipped and trained for, or interested in.

Circumstantial insecurity is simply not feeling secure in the moment. Once the moment or situation has passed, you are not left with lingering adverse feelings or reactions to what has happened. You do not walk away with anxiety or a decrease in your self-worth. Even if this were an area you believed you possessed the ability to fill the need, but fell short, your level of understanding and comfort regarding who you are as a person will determine your response to it, and how you feel once the moment has passed. When we struggle with characteristic insecurity, it is usually circumstantial insecurity that causes feelings of uncertainty to surface and operate in our hearts and minds. This is the unhealthy insecurity. The only good that could possibly come from this, is the ability to recognize it's there and doesn't belong.

3

CHARACTERISTIC INSECURITY

"I think my biggest flaw is my insecurity. I'm terribly insecure. I'm plagued with insecurities 24/7." - Madonna

In order to lay the foundation for Characteristic insecurity, let's again touch basis on a few definitions that relate to it.

INSECURITY
    1.) lack of confidence or assurance; self-doubt
    2.) the quality or state of being insecure

INSECURE
    1.) subject to fears, doubts, etc.; not self-confident or assured
    2.) not confident or certain; uneasy; anxious
    3.) not secure; exposed or liable to risk, loss, or danger
    4.) not firmly or reliably placed or fastened

SECURE
    1.) free from fear or distrust
    2.) ease of mind
    3.) assured in opinion or expectation; having no doubt
    4.) free from danger, risk, or loss; safety

I would like to summarize the definition of insecurity as the sum of our belief system and its mental resolves. Based on what we believe, we determine what is stable or unstable. Insecurity is the emotional feeling resulting from the evaluation of a thing as unsure, unstable, or unsafe—the thing calling for our interaction, involvement, commitment, or trust. When we resolve that something is not sure, true, stable, or safe, we often feel apprehensive about it. Being forced to go around these feelings, typically results in increased fear.

In the previous chapter, I shed light on circumstantial insecurity, and my belief that it is the most natural and healthy form of insecurity that one may experience. Characteristic insecurity does not carry the same positive possibilities. It's damaging from start to finish. EVERY poor decision I've ever made can be traced back to the presence of characteristic insecurity. It is the most debilitating, paralyzing, and negative form of insecurity. It may be the reason you are reading this book. I don't know a person plagued with the latter form, who is genuinely happy and at peace. They may experience spurts of joy, but these spurts are always short-lived due to the constant rise of insecurity and its accompanying feelings of fear, anxiety, doubt, and inadequacy. It can go from being quiet and unassuming, to loud and aggressive, all in one minute. It dominates our thoughts and sends our emotions into a state of instability. It becomes the filter by which we process most things in life. With fear as its fuel, we shrink into intimidation as we anticipate criticism and judgment.

As we take steps to clearly understand this type of insecurity, let's first consider the dictionary definition of *character*, which is the root word in *characteristic*.

CHARACTER
1) The aggregate of features and traits that form the individual nature of some person or thing.
2) One such feature or trait; characteristic
3) Moral or ethical quality
4) Qualities of honesty, courage, or the like; integrity
5) Reputation
6) Good repute
7) An account of the qualities or peculiarities of a person or thing.
8) A person, especially with reference to behavior or personality

Our character is a combination of characteristics (qualities) used to describe who we are as people. It is a reflection of our identity, and how we identify. Identity is the truth of who someone is as an individual. It's how we are identified physically, mentally, and spiritually. It consists of our unique physical traits, such as our finger prints and DNA, all the way down to very personal life experiences and beliefs. It is the source of what we are connected to and what we pull from to know who we are and where we belong.

Character or characteristics, describe(s) who a person is. Characteristic insecurity is the type of insecurity that is part of your character. As stated before, character is a reflection of your identity.

Circumstantial insecurity is hosted by *life*. Characteristic insecurity is hosted by a *person*. Circumstantial insecurity is short-lived. Characteristic insecurity is constant. It becomes the difference in saying, "That made me feel insecure," and "I feel insecure." One visits, the other abides. The one that abides walks in, unpacks its bags, and stays. It is part of your make-up. It is one of the characteristics that reflects YOU. The way a person can be described as strong, pretty, angry, talented, bitter, happy, peaceful, tall, or short, all things that describe physical and mental qualities, can also be said of characteristic insecurity. Once it begins to operate in your life, it becomes an appropriate description of who you are as a person.

In discussing character, we must note how it is commonly spoken of. A person is often described as having or not having character. Also, character is typically spoken of as a favorable thing. Let's consider this example: "Bob is a man of character." In this sentence, the assumption is that Bob's character is good, as it is a common intention of people to use it as a favorable descriptor. This common assumption eliminates the critical thinking necessary to consider that the aforementioned sentence may also be suggesting that the character Bob has consists of negatives. The truth is, ALL people have character because all people have identity. If identity has been conceived with some amount of negative ingredients, a portion of one's character will reveal negativity. Again, character is the product of identity. It will always reflect who or what we have come to identity with as individuals.

Every person on earth has a unique set of fingerprints. Even those born in multiples have been created with different sets of fingerprints. Without ever seeing a person's face, hearing their voice, or knowing their name, you can scan their fingerprints and identify who they are by their unique DNA. Our identities determine how we are recognized. Identity is also a mirror that reflects what we have identified with. Each facet of our identities help reveal who we are. Identity is created and shaped by our belief system and life experiences that have worked together to produce the thoughts we feel about God, life, and ourselves. Our social interaction, the things we value, our passions, what we love, what we hate, what we pursue, and ultimately WHO WE ARE, are all ingredients of our identities. What we identify with is most often associated with what we believe. We then build character based on what we identify with. Character is then manifested through our personalities. The most common sign of characteristic insecurity is not what a person thinks, but what they do. Our personalities and outputs are great reflections of what's going on inside of us. An accurate account of what a person believes cannot be assessed by only listening to what they profess; it is far more accurate to look at what they do. "For as a he thinks within himself, so is he" (*New American Standard Bible, Prov. 23.7*). We're directed by what's inside of us. We are what's inside of us.

Human beings have been given the ability to walk in self-control. As a result, many of us have learned how to control or manipulate our actions, behavior, and reactions. Sometimes this includes actions, behavior, and reactions that are contrary to our character. Our character, in its rawest form, has natural responses that are innate, and don't need to be controlled, manipulated or monitored. These actions speak of who we are. But when working to reflect character that is not ours, we must respond in ways contrary to who we are. It requires concentration, an abnormal amount of self-manipulation, reflection, study of what one who naturally possesses the quality is like, and an overly aware disposition to our surroundings. It isn't necessarily a bad thing to be able to give responses outside of our natural development. In some cases, it is a vital part of social interaction. I've worked in the hospitality industry for the last 15 years. Dealing with difficult clients and customers often requires a controlled and professional response, instead of the one that "Shaunee off the clock" would give. I have also found this to be a useful quality in being a pastor, alongside my husband. My natural disposition is kind, friendly, and professional, but on a day where my temperament is tested, there is another side that would LOVE to pop out. She is sarcastic, blunt, and curt. She's the one who, when pushed and disrespected by rude and spoiled members of the general population, will tell them to duct tape their traps. She's a work in progress. Please pray for her. She doesn't seem to want to go anywhere.

My professional experiences provide examples of me being able to choose what I would reflect. Our characteristics ultimately reflect our level of self-control and discipline; however, it's unfortunate when we begin behaving in ways outside of our norms, in an effort to reflect characteristics we don't possess and benefit momentarily, instead of working to build our identities and benefit permanently. Good character cannot be borrowed—it can only be developed or depicted by acting. To imitate qualities that do not belong to us for the sake of benefiting and being accepted, makes us frauds. It ultimately reflects that we have given up on one or more of the following ideas: 1.) We should change 2.) We can change 3.) It's worth changing for. Many of us are afraid of what change will require of us and whether or not we can maintain it all.

Journal Moment

Consider the definition of character. What do you believe determines your character? First start by journaling the things YOU believe make up your character, using as many descriptors or thoughts necessary. Next, write the ways others have described your character.

Now, write the things you believe make up your identity. What or who do you identify with? Be honest and reflective. If you need to take time to think about it first, do that. Remember, this is YOUR journal. This is for you. No one else is reading this; you are free to be butt-naked (totally transparent) on these pages. Smile.

THE FUEL OF FEAR

"It has always seemed that a fear of judgement is the mark of guilt, and the burden of insecurity."
- Criss Jami

When characteristic insecurity operates in our lives, it becomes the filter by which we process most things. A simple dinner invitation can elicit feelings of anxiety almost immediately, as a person may start worrying beforehand about what to wear, and how they'll be viewed or accepted once they get there. Maybe not receiving a dinner invitation at all would leave someone with feelings of rejection or assumptions as to why they were not invited, and conclusions derived from their own understanding, or lack thereof. At the end of it all, whether or not an invitation to dinner was extended, there are feelings of fear that reside within the person. Sometimes the fear is small, while at other times it's massive. Still, it's always fear in some form. At the root of this insecurity is the fear of judgment, rejection, criticism, and exposure. It's the fear that everything you believe to be true about yourself will be seen—the things you work hard to hide or to fix. It's exhausting to keep your feelings hidden, but even more exhausting worrying about what will happen if you fail. People and life events trigger these feelings, and once triggered, fear is what feeds them.

We wrestle with thoughts due to over-analyzing, in an attempt to reach a place of calm, peace, and acceptance. This is because the roots of our insecurities are based on thinking that comes from our beliefs. We usually settle on external things to calm the storm, instead of finding truth to change our beliefs. We rely on temporary fixes to deal with the symptoms, instead of a cure to kill the disease. We utilize a wide variety of coping mechanisms (discussed in a later chapter) and tactics to manipulate situations, people, and our feelings, in order to get through these moments. Most people struggle to change what they believe. It's often difficult to get around deep-rooted memories, theological beliefs, and life experiences, that have greatly affected our courses of life. It takes time, openness, submission, humility, and healing. Our impatience as a society looks to shortcut this process. We are more interested in the moment, as opposed to sacrifice that secures a future. When fear surfaces, the discomfort of it is overwhelming. It takes power over our thoughts, nervous system, and even our heart rate. In this case, a normal pattern of thinking is out of reach. Once we arrive at this point, we are not interested in a cure by process. We're more apt to simply medicate. The problem with satisfying symptoms, as opposed to curing them, is that when the symptoms subside, we believe there is no longer a problem. However, once the medication wears off, the symptoms return and we are reminded that the problem is still there.

Fear, pain, and discomfort are ways that our bodies and minds alert us to problems or possible danger. Problems or potential danger cannot always be perceived correctly—our beliefs are the determinants of how we perceive things. If a false belief is directing one's perception, their perception is likely false. But as mentioned before, "truth" that is false, *IS* still truth to the one who perceives it as such. We will always live by what we believe is true. The only way to correctly perceive problems and potential danger, is to have a foundation of truth shaping our beliefs. What we believe to be untrue, is the result of what we believe to be true. Truth always comes first—it is what we know, not what we don't know, that directs us.

Many quote Hosea 4:6 which says, "…people are destroyed for lack of knowledge" *(NASB)*. It is the belief that what we don't know is the cause of our ruin. The truth is, however, what we don't know is never an issue until we set out to do something that requires *that* knowledge. It becomes an issue when what we *do* know is not enough for what we are trying to accomplish. A lack of knowledge doesn't become a problem until you need the knowledge you don't have to do something that requires it. Me not knowing how to rewire the entire electrical system in my house is not an issue. I have absolutely no knowledge as to where to start or what to do, and have never had a need to know. However, it becomes a huge issue once I've torn down the walls, ceiling, and light sockets to set out to do it myself. Most of us are trying to get through life and deal with fear and insecurities, with limited knowledge. The limited knowledge takes away our ability to make sound judgments. It allows fear to have full reign through our insecurities. It's like cuddling with a snake, but running for your life when you see a kitten. In so many words, we just don't know better.

I was standing in the bathroom, doing my makeup and getting ready to leave. Haven, my four-year-old, was in there with me, invading my privacy, as usual. She rambled on, and on, and on, talking about everything from face paint, to roller skates. She was talking so much and I was so busy getting ready, that I failed to give her my full attention. Then I noticed her speech become spaced out, then she became entirely quiet. I glanced at her quickly and was absolutely horrified. Little Miss Haven had grabbed one of my bobby pins, and was jamming it in the light socket.

SWEET……HOLY…….BABY……JESUS.

I snapped just a little bit. The combination of motherly protectiveness, complete disbelief at the fact that this is what her little buns had been standing there doing, and that irritated confusion parents feel when their children are doing something completely ridiculous, all flooded me at once. I snatched the bobby pin out of her hand and popped her forehead, the closest thing to me, a couple of times. I stunned her and could feel my face twisted and likely glaring. She started crying, and I felt my nervous system cooling down.

"Haven!!! Don't you ever, ever, EVER do that again!" I yelled. On several occasions my husband and I have had to coach Haven into trying new things because she was afraid. We had to coach her at the water park, the zoo, and concerning certain characters on TV that posed absolutely no danger to her, but that had scared her into apprehensive tendencies, and even immobility. It would be a certain amount of time between us explaining to her that something was harmless, and her comprehending and eventually testing the truth we'd revealed to her. She didn't just take our word for it, she had to be sure for herself. But here she was, the one afraid of things that were harmless, getting ready to electrocute her eyeballs out of their sockets. This is the result of limited knowledge. She does not yet know the potential danger of improperly combining electricity and metal. Her limited knowledge was not a problem until she attempted to do something that required this knowledge.

This is often what makes fear possible. Remember, I stated at the very beginning of this journey that, "You will never outgrow insecurity. It is only something that you can out-know." It is impossible to make sound-minded, accurate decisions with fear, it's illusions, and deceptions present. The basis of most of our insecurities, especially characteristic insecurity, is the fear that we will be judged. Some would consider people as the triggers of these fears, but people would not be an issue if the fear did not exist in the first place. The reality is, people never have to criticize us—we criticize ourselves. We become insecure by our own observations of ourselves and how we believe the observations have summarized our worth and value. Living with these unhealthy thoughts and feelings cause us to be oversensitive to the likelihood that other people notice them as well. People cannot tap into feelings that do not already exist, nor can they plant them without soil that has already been fertilized with other insecure

32

thoughts. Even if no one else were present, we would still have to live with ourselves, and for those of us who struggle with insecurity, we undergo a continuous process of rehearsing negative feelings about ourselves throughout the day. We wake up in the morning and lie down at night with them. People are only able to confirm or deny what we already believe about ourselves. Without our conscious or subconscious agreement, what others think of us is hardly ever a factor.

SAUL – THE LEAST OF THEM

"We each appear to hold within ourselves a range of divergent views as to our native qualities. And amid such uncertainty, we typically turn to the wider world to settle the question of our significance. We seem beholden to affections of others to endure ourselves." - Alain de Botton

There was a season where I had come out of great failure. I was in the process of healing and gaining truth concerning God and His restorative heart. I'd read the story of Saul and David many times, but it's something about being broken that opens up your understanding in a different way. The humility that comes from failure, followed by accepting God's goodness, creates a blank canvas for Him to draw on. Around this time, I was licking my wounds after a season of hurt caused by my insecurities—the ones that had nearly destroyed my life. As I began reading the story of Saul and David, I yearned for the knowledge of acceptance David walked in. I also saw much of myself in Saul; for the first time, I actually had a sense of compassion for him.

God never wanted Israel to have a king. He always wanted the people to see Him as their king, and for their hearts to be turned toward Him. Yet, in their desire to be like other nations, they demanded that God give them a king, too. Considering their hearts, God gave them the type of king they asked for—He gave them Saul. The people served as a catalyst—the reason a "king" had become a factor in the first place. God was against it, but He decided to use the desires of the people's hearts to bring forth a king.

"There was a man of Benjamin whose name was Kish, the son of Abiel, son of Zeror, son of Becorath, son of Aphiah, a Benjaminite, a man of wealth. And he had a son whose name was Saul, a handsome young man. There was not a man among the people of Israel more

33

handsome than he. From his shoulders upward he was taller than any of the people" (English Standard Version, 1 Sam. 9.1-2).

God searched their hearts, and knew that appearance was a major criterion. It mattered to them. So he searched all the tribes and found Saul. The bible says:

"So they ran and took him from there, and when he stood among the people, he was taller than any of the people from his shoulders upward. Samuel said to all the people, 'Do you see him whom the LORD has chosen? Surely there is no one like him among all the people.' So all the people shouted and said, 'Long live the king!'" (NASB, 1 Sam. 10. 23-24).

He'd given them just what they'd asked for, from both their mouths and hearts. However, Saul's response to being chosen reflects the very thing that would be his downfall—his insecurity.

"But as for your donkeys that were lost three days ago, do not be anxious about them, for they have been found. And on whom is all the desire of Israel? Is it not on you and on all your father's house?" And Saul answered and said, 'Am I not a Benjamite, of the smallest of the tribes of Israel, and my family the least of all the families of the tribe of Benjamin? Why then do you speak like this to me?'" (New King James Version,1 Sam. 9.20-21).

Saul's belief concerning his worth was very poor as a result of his cultural and familial upbringing. Since his tribe was classified as the smallest, they lacked in economic respect and recognition, which caused their pride to take a hit. Not to mention, Saul's family was the smallest family of the smallest tribe. During Saul's time, tribe and family status determined economic status, respect, and recognition. In essence, his family was the poorest, and least esteemed family in the entire nation. If we compare Saul's situation to a situation in today's society, it would be equivalent to America needing a president, and choosing a man living out of a cardboard box to run the Oval Office. Saul was born and raised with a poverty-stricken mentality. He had been reared with the knowledge that his family was less than; he was told this his entire life. This mindset shaped his view of himself. He had come to accept and expect that this would always be his fate. He'd settled in this mentality. He had no expectation for anything different. So imagine when Samuel showed up and told Saul he had been chosen to fulfill the most important role in his nation. The first thing to come out of his mouth likely mirrored his own thoughts, and expectations: "Who am I? Why me? I am the least of them all." Here it was, a nation of insecure people who felt they needed a physical king to measure up to other nations, was receiving an insecure leader. The bible even states that when they went to get Saul to anoint him, he was hiding! At no point did he think he was fit to be king, even after Samuel told him God had chosen him for such a position. It was not enough to change his thoughts concerning himself.

Saul became king, which fulfilled every prophecy and warning God had given the people beforehand, about not choosing a king over Him. The entire time he ruled, Saul lived to please the people. His insecurities did not vanish with power or esteem; in fact, they were magnified. For the first time in his life, he was someone of importance. But he knew he was there at the request of the people. The people had promoted Saul, therefore, the people owned him. For this reason, Saul ruled with the people in mind, even if it meant defying God.

God gave Saul this order:

"Now go, attack the Amalekites and totally destroy all that belongs to them. Do not spare them; put to death men and women, children and infants, cattle and sheep, camels and donkeys" (New International Version, 1 Sam. 15.3).

Saul and his army went and destroyed the Amalekites, but did not obey the entire order. Not only did they keep the women and children, they kept the cattle and spoils as well. God spoke to Samuel and told him that because of Saul's disobedience, he would be rejected and God would raise up another king. When Samuel confronted Saul about his disobedience, he tried justifying his decision first. This is a common trait in people who are fearful and insecure. As previously mentioned, such people will gladly take medication, rather than receiving the cure. Justification typically seems more convenient than taking responsibility, and is meant to buy time and acceptance. Still, Samuel refused to accept Saul's disobedience, but was able to get to the root of what made Saul defy God, who chose him to fulfill the people's need.

"Then Saul admitted to Samuel, 'Yes, I have sinned. I have disobeyed your instructions and the LORD's command, for I was afraid of the people and did what they demanded. But now, please forgive my sin and come back with me so that I may worship the LORD'" (New Living Translation, 1 Sam. 15.24-25).

The root of Saul's decision was a fear of the people. People had caused his promotion, therefore, people had his focus—God was secondary. Saul's opinion of himself long before becoming king, followed him all the way to the throne. It was a thought concerning his worth that made the fear of people possible. Ultimately, the fear that he would lose the people's affection, cost him the throne he'd used to gain it. His insecurity was not satisfied by position—it simply morphed into a more dormant status that surfaced when triggered. Those who are insecure will typically follow the path of acceptance. Their actions tell where they have identified most. Saul's identity was rooted in acceptance from people, instead of acceptance from God. This is what made it possible for people's desires to trump God's, regarding the choices Saul made. Knowing the right decision to make was not enough, his fear of rejection overpowered the truth of what was required. His insecurities didn't change simply because his position did. The same insecurities Saul believed disqualified him from birth, were the same insecurities that made it possible for the people he should have been ruling, to rule him.

DAVID – THE LAST OF THEM

"The Lord is my Shepherd. I shall not want." - Psalm 23:1, NASB

Let's also consider David; he and Saul came from similar situations. David's economic status was not quite the same, but his placement within his family was the least respected and most underestimated. As the youngest of his brothers, David was technically last in line for the inheritance. It was both order and custom of his time, for age to be considered in regard to promotion within a family. When God spoke to Samuel to tell him Saul would be replaced, He gave him very specific directions that a son of Jesse's house would be anointed the new king. He did not give Samuel any other instructions other than to go, and that He would show him which one would be king. But Samuel, a man of God, called by God, made the mistake that people, no matter their purpose here in the earth, often make; he leaned to his own understanding to make a decision.

When Jesse and his sons came before Samuel, the bible says:

"When they arrived, Samuel saw Eliab and thought, 'the Lord's anointed stands here before the Lord.' But the Lord said to Samuel, 'Do not consider his appearance or his height, for I have rejected him. The Lord does not look at the things people look at. People look at the outward appearance, but the Lord looks at the heart'" (NIV, 1 Sam. 16.6-7).

Using the same criteria used to pick Saul, Samuel assumed that Eliab was the correct the choice. Eliab was the oldest of the brothers, and likely the largest and most developed. Of them all, I am almost certain that by appearance, he looked the most mature. But God being God, He checked Samuel quick.

Let me translate Samuel and God's conversation above:

SAMUEL: "Oooooo.......God......he's niiiiice isn't he? Good choice! Good choice.... nice broad shoulders, tall, dark hair. Yes, he'd be a fine king. Let me know when to swab a little oil on his forehead. I'm ready. He's glowing and everything!"

GOD: "Um..........no sir. Samuel, hush. I know how we did it before, but not this time. Stop looking at his appearance and stature, none of that amounts to a hill of beans. I'm not like you or anyone else; I'm doing the choosing this time. You all look at what's on the outside—I'm looking at the heart. He's not the one. Now keep looking."

According to custom, because of Eliab's age, he was a shoe in for the birthright—first to be considered. Yet, God had already considered him and all the others who'd come before David, and all of them had been rejected. The bible goes on to say that Jesse brought an additional seven sons before Samuel, all of which God told Samuel were not His choice. It wasn't until all of the options were presented, that David even became a choice.

"So he asked Jesse, 'Are these all the sons you have?' 'There is still the youngest,' Jesse answered. 'He is tending the sheep.' Samuel said, 'Send for him; we will not sit down until he arrives.' So he sent for him and had him brought in. He was glowing with health and had a fine appearance and handsome features. Then the LORD said, 'Rise and anoint him; this is the one'" (NIV, 1 Sam. 16.11-12).

Samuel anointed David on the spot, in front of all his brothers. The youngest, the last in line, was now God's choice to lead them all. UNHEARD OF. Beforehand, David had been given the least worthy job of tending to the sheep. But it was in the wilderness and solitude—in the company of sheep, that David became one with the Lord. It was there, in the lowest position, where he was rejected by people, that he found acceptance from God. This is where he was developed. This was the difference between Saul and David: both were positioned and shaped by rejection, but one ran to people for affirmation—the other ran to God.

"Though my mother and my father forsake me, the Lord will receive me."
- Psalm 27:10, NIV

David went on to become king and lead the people of Israel as he'd been anointed to do. But the story of David defeating Goliath, also included another giant that is often overlooked. David was sent by his father to the battlefield to look after his older brothers who had been sent there for battle. In spite of his anointing, David had returned to doing menial jobs for the family. He was going to the battlefield as an errand boy.

In so many words, this is what David's family said to him:

"Whelp, David, it's great that the prophet was here and everything—good for you! Uh…now go wipe that oil off of your forehead and get back out there into the wilderness before some of the sheep run off. Oh, and before you go, don't forget to feed the chickens, and clean out the pigs' pen and horses' stables."

They didn't give a rat's tail WHO he'd been anointed to be. To them, he was still "Little ol' David." In a day and time where men dominated, it's probable that David was teased and bullied by his brothers because he was the youngest. Family is family—they are sometimes the most precious, beautiful, and safest parts of our lives, at other times, they can be downright terrible, and a constant reminder of things we'd like to forget. They are the most familiar with us. They know things about us that others don't. Family can sometimes be the last to respect us or consider our worth and potential, because they are often most familiar with our issues, and easily overlook valuable qualities. The opinions of our family members matter, but not when what they think, contradicts what God thinks. We cannot allow anyone's opinion of us to keep us from fulfilling potential. Please remember this.

So, David was sent to the battlefield for a completely different job, but stumbled upon purpose. He'd gone there to serve. His heart of service is what positioned him to conquer. He had not let his anointing deceive him into believing that he was no longer a servant. Goliath requested an opponent from the army of Israel, just like he'd done every day before, believing he'd leave without anyone coming forth. In other words, the entire army, including Saul, was scared out of their minds, shaking in their boots. Goliath had scared the drawers off each of them. But here comes David— "Little ol' David," whose only job was to watch the sheep. The little errand boy just so happened to be present when Goliath showed up. David, the one who had spent many days and nights in the wilderness, with sheep and God. David, who had been rescued from the lion and the bear. David, who, during his wilderness moments, had come to know the reality of God and His love for him. Goliath was a joke to him—he was no match for his God. David felt indignation at the thought of someone challenging his FRIEND! It was personal! David was going to handle it himself.

But first, he had to defeat a different giant. He had to get past the very thing that had sought to hold him back by custom, birthright, intimidation, and evil reminders—he had to get past his eldest brother, Eliab.

"When Eliab, David's oldest brother, heard him speaking with the men, he burned with anger at him and asked, 'Why have you come down here? And with whom did you leave those few sheep in the wilderness? I know how conceited you are and how wicked your heart is; you came down only to watch the battle'" (NIV, 1 Sam. 17.28).

In David's eyes, Eliab represented a status. He represented memories of being forgotten and rejected by family—those who should have been the first to accept him. Eliab, the oldest and most valued, represented the lifelong reminder that David was the last, and least. Eliab was there to remind David of his responsibility to do the lowest job in the family—the job that required no talent, skill or strength. Eliab's goal was to remind David that all these things defined him, and that they ALWAYS would. The truth is, Eliab was holding a grudge. Eliab was angry, jealous, and intimidated. As the oldest and first in line for the birthright, he had not forgotten the day the prophet showed up and anointed his baby brother, David, instead. David, who he'd never viewed as a threat to his position, had taken the place that belonged to him. He had spent years thinking about it. He never forgot the day his spot was given away, and that there was nothing he could do to redeem it. This was not man's choice, but God's. Eliab's hands were tied. Having been rejected and with his pride hurt, he made David his target. Considering David's history, Eliab was a far greater giant than Goliath. Goliath opposed the nation, but Eliab opposed the destiny of the future king of *that* nation. David did not defeat Eliab that day. It had happened long before that day in the wilderness, where it was just David, the sheep, and God.

CONCLUSION

Characteristic insecurity, in all its glory, isn't glorious at all. The effort to satisfy this type of insecurity, becomes a lifetime task. Its ability to lie dormant and disguise itself as other qualities, makes it difficult to tame. The idea that it eventually goes away on its own, is one of the many misconceptions that keep people bound to it. The saying "time heals all wounds" sounds good, but is absolutely false. In fact, if not confronted, time further exposes the wounds. A bitter older person and a bitter younger person are often notably different. Similar to the potency of fine, aged wine, is the bitterness of aged wounds. Insecurity that has had time to brew, has also had time to grow in strength, power, and influence. At some point, we employ so many coping mechanisms that we become deceived by insecurity's ability to mask itself. Time alone cannot heal a wound. Understanding, clarity, and a change of perspective, given by God and life experiences is the thing that will heal a wound.

Confronting insecurity is such a personal and necessary task for anyone dealing with it. Each person's approach is customized to their life's experiences. In order to see insecurity for what it is, we must first look at how it operates. If you are able to spot the signs, you are better able to determine its presence. Discovery is the key to change.

Journal Moment

Do you see any similarities to yourself in Saul and David? Do you believe that characteristic insecurity is an issue that you need to tackle?

Hi Insecurity. BYE Insecurity.

4

SYMPTOMS & COPING MECHANISMS

"I'm always described as 'cocksure' or 'with a swagger', and that bears no resemblance to who I feel like inside. I feel plagued by insecurity."
- Ben Affleck

If you haven't yet asked yourself the question, "Am I insecure?" we need to stop right here. I'm not worried about the answer, it's beside the point right now. Not being able to ask yourself the question is the real problem; it's a sign of a bigger issue. An inability to self-evaluate and be open to a possibility you may have never been exposed to, is a sign of one of three things: fear, pride, or ignorance. After reading all you have thus far, you owe it to yourself. Maybe you still don't know the answer, or maybe you're still afraid to ask it. Maybe you've already answered "yes," but do not know to which degree it has affected your life.

We do not know we're hosting sickness or disease in our bodies until we start experiencing the symptoms associated with it. When we go to the doctor, it's usually because of something we're seeing or feeling outside of the normal functioning of our bodies. We do not go in and say, "Hi, doctor. I'm feeling cancer." We usually go in and describe symptoms of pain or other abnormal signs that denote the presence of a problem. Using our symptoms, the doctor is typically able to narrow down the possibilities in order to know what to test for.

Since insecurity is an illness for many people, we have to treat it the same way. You are the patient and you'll need to describe your symptoms. You may be sitting thinking: *There's nothing wrong with me. I feel perfectly normal.* Guess what, that's one of the symptoms. An inability to self-evaluate, answering questions prior to receiving all the information necessary to give an accurate answer, then believing there is nothing more to learn because you already "know it all," are signs of suppression and denial. Human beings have been gifted to adapt. We typically find ways to deal with hindrances, rather than removing them. Sometimes, after we've lived with an abnormality for so long, it becomes a normal part of who we are, especially because we never truly realize how much more we can accomplish and become in its absence.

An illness or abnormality is diagnosed as such based on what it takes from us, even if by adding something far more detrimental. It is classified by a deficiency, and like with any deficiency, we seek to regain what is lost with a cure. If a cure is not readily available, we supplement to fill the need. The deficiencies of insecurity are extensive and vast; however, most, if not all of them, result in feelings of inadequacy, discomfort, and anxiety. When these symptoms arise, we create our own supplements or attempt to self-medicate, in an effort to make the feelings associated with them, subside. It is common to make life-altering decisions, not just momentary ones, to escape our feelings of insecurity. Since we equate security with peace, we work to secure what we believe will provide us with peace, even if these things are only temporary fixes. This process is effective in the moment, but ineffective in the long run. The problem with supplementing/self-medicating in dealing with insecurity, is that we typically use external, temporal, perishable, artificial, and circumstantial things, to make ourselves feel better. When we use these things as supplements, we work even harder to make them work, as they require a certain level of maintenance to guarantee their effectiveness.

When I first got married, Gayle and I would lay up at night watching different television shows. One night I stumbled across an *Intervention* marathon on A&E. The next day they had the nerve to follow it up with a *Hoarders* marathon. For some reason it had me hooked, much to the annoyance of Gayle. I was absolutely fascinated with the mentalities of people who were either hooked on substances, or hoarding things in their home, to the point of eviction or the home being condemned. I was mesmerized by the measures they'd taken to dull their pain. Most of them had been doing it so long, they'd somehow become oblivious to the cause of their behavior. I would watch for hours and hours, popcorn in hand, eyes glued.

"Why are you watching this again? Okay, I'm not watching this again tonight!" Gayle would say. Having grown up with a father who suffered from alcoholism, the stories reminded Gayle of an issue that still hit too close to home. I'd also grown up with a grandmother who suffered from alcoholism. I witnessed many moments where she was intoxicated to the point of having split personalities. Through watching these shows, I'd received a greater understanding of how both Gayle's father and my grandmother processed life's hurts, shaping them into dysfunction. With every story, whether they involved substance abuse or hoarding, each person experienced trauma, leaving them in a state of mental and emotional insecurity. For these people, substance abuse and hoarding were forms of supplementation.

Supplements for insecurity come in many different forms, including the form of people. Honestly, there is nothing worse than "needing" people to help you feel better about yourself. People are the most unstable and "moody" supplements available. Love and recognition given by people can sway like the wind, depending on your performance level in comparison to their expectations. Many times you end up on a constant roller coaster of worry and apprehension, afraid of how others perceive you. Human supplementation is one of the most exhausting forms and, in some cases, can be the most damaging. Many people have become addicted to social media outlets, not out of the need for social interaction, but more so the need for social recognition. They paint lives and stories that help them gain recognition or acceptance through an image, as opposed to reality. It is also a readily available distraction to help one avoid dealing with both internal and external issues. No matter how we choose to supplement, in the end, its effects eventually fade, leaving us to, once again, attempt to combat insecurity and all its fruit.

If you are in denial or simply unaware of what insecurity looks like while in operation, as we explore the subtle and overt characteristics, personality types, and emotional outputs that accompany it, you will gain more clarity. Hopefully it will help you self-evaluate more effectively.

SO I LIED

"The inconvenient thing about truth, is that it cannot be manipulated. There is only one version, and that version produces freedom. This is offensive to the one looking for a way to stay chained." - Shaunee Brannan

I was eight years old and we were all huddled on top of the oversized, red bean bag in the gymnasium equipment room. We laughed and smiled in between gasps of air, trying to catch our breath from jumping for 15 minutes straight. The question was posed, "So what did you get for Christmas?" Each girl took turns running down a list of items, and with every new voice that spoke, I started coming to a very alarming realization—I was different, and it would soon be my turn to speak. They talked about receiving video games, new clothing, expensive shoes, toys from grandma, and money from mom, but this had been one of the scarcest Christmases my family had ever had; yet, the truth of that had not been illuminated until this moment. The reality of how little we'd received could not be measured until there was a point of comparison. I didn't REALLY know my parents didn't have much money until then.

Right before it was my turn, Felicia spoke. Felicia was the popular one. She was the one all the other girls gravitated to. She was quiet and friendly, but she was cute—VERY cute. She was light-skinned, with long hair and beautiful slanted eyes. To top it off, she and her older sister, who was equally as cute, ALWAYS dressed really nice, in the latest and greatest attire.

While others excitedly told what they had gotten for Christmas, I reminisced on how, a week before, we were all lined up at the back of the gym, and all the boys in our class were making known who they "liked," as we called it. You know who they thought was cute. They'd all pretty much chosen Felicia, though several opted to give secondary choices in the event that Felicia didn't have a reciprocal response. Those little turdy boys knew, even at an early age, how to run game on us girls. A couple of them chose me as a secondary choice, but only one of them chose me as his first option. It was Reginald, the one with the chapped lips and snot around his nostrils that had caught a little wind and crusted up, and who had the most obnoxious laugh, similar to the squeal of a pubescent seal. I was NOT flattered. He was the crossing guard assistant on my street corner, and I had to walk past him every day on my way to school. He teased me often and pushed me on occasion. He was much bigger than me and I couldn't stand him. That's why when, with a sheepish grin on his face, a fluctuating diverted stare, and battering eyelashes, he finally said my name, I looked him directly in his eyeballs and stuck my tongue out with so much exertion and for so long, that it completely dried up. That was the best way I knew to express to him how I TRULY felt, without coming out and saying, "No sir!!! Me no likey you!"

As I shifted my focus back to my present situation, it was Felicia's turn, and listened intently to her spout off her list of treasures.

"Well…I got a baby doll, and these shoes," she said, pointing at a brand new pair of purple and white Nikes. "…and a video game, and…" Her list never ended. As all of us girls gazed at her in envy, amazement, and with a great desire to be her friend, if not her completely, she turned to me and asked, "Yoshaundala…So what did you get?'

I came out of my gaze to find several sets of eyes looking at me intently, waiting for me to run down my list—only I didn't have one. I thought about the skirts my mother made for me and my sister, then, *NO, not cool enough.* I thought to mention the UNO game my siblings and I had gotten…TO SHARE, and I realized, *Nope, not good.* What about the card game—I ended that thought before I could finish it because it definitely wasn't cool enough. I thought a few gifts, like the the no-name plastic baby doll, would be cool to mention, but most of the other girls had already mentioned they'd gotten Barbie and Baby Alive dolls, with all the matching accessories.

GOD! Why do I have to go right after Felecia? I thought.
As they sat waiting, I opened my mouth and I decided right then and there, TO LIE! I ran down a list of elaborate items, mostly including things the other girls had said. They all "oooh'd" and "ahhhh'd" at my list, staring in amazement and nodding in approval. I even mentioned receiving a new pair of Nike's, making sure to mention that they were "…just like yours Felecia! But my mom said that I couldn't wear them to school. She don't want me getting them dirty on the playground, so I wear these, my play shoes."

I was referring to my pair of lavender, Velcro strapped, Jordache running shoes. Nearly a month before my current interrogation, my dad and mom were having a discussion about my sister and me needing shoes. He'd expressed that he didn't want my mom to take us, because she was a spender. She was a stay-at-home mom of four children and occasionally sold Tupperware or Avon for a little extra spending money, but nothing significant enough to help pay bills. She was a full-time homemaker, that was her job. We were living on one income, the entry-level pay my father received as a fireman for the Detroit Fire Department. Later he retired as Captain, with 34 years of service under his belt. However, at the time I generated a list of made-up gifts, my dad's pay had to be in the range of $33,000 a year. He never called off work, sick or not, and by no means was he the type to slack off while there. He utilized every penny he made in an effort to tackle debt and support the immediate needs of his family. Wants were always secondary and occasional. Requests for McDonald's or White Castle were always met with, "I got you some McDonald's all right... I'll fix you a peanut butter and jelly when we get home." The idea of sending my mom to the store to buy us shoes was too chancy, in my dad's opinion. She'd grown up with very nice things and they had gotten married right out of high school. Her concept of money was based on how it had always been given to her and not how hard it was to come by. There was a great possibility that she'd take us to the store and come back with something we couldn't afford. So my dad said, "Tee, I'll take care of it," before bundling my sister and me up and loading us in the front seat of his pick-up truck. We drove for about 3 miles before he pulled into the local Big Lots. "Okay, get out girls," he said.

"Daddy, what are we here for?" I asked in confusion.

"To get your shoes," he replied. This was a first.

We didn't get many clothes aside from what my mother made us, but at the beginning of the school year, my dad always made sure to buy us one nice, brand-name pair of shoes from a department store. He consistently made sure we understood that the shoes were meant to last the entire year; however, we were both growing so fast that we were in need of new shoes prior to the end of the year. I didn't know much about our economic status, but I did know we'd recently been enrolled back into a public school from a private institution. This was caused by the added financial strain of paying tuition for three children. My ignorance regarding my family's economic status was being revealed to me as I walked into Big Lots, gathering that this was the best my parents could do. As we gazed at the shoes hanging from racks by their white strings instead of being boxed, my heart sank knowing that we wouldn't be getting anything trendy. My dad sat us both on a counter, tried the shoes on us, made us stand up, and said, "Wiggle your big toe." He was trying to measure the amount of space our feet took up inside the shoe.

"Okay, Shaunee, these will work," he said. Next, he had my sister try on a rainbow pair, which was an even bigger nightmare. They looked like they'd been made out of a vat of rainbow sherbet. I studied her face intently, trying to get an idea of how she felt about them. I could tell from her body language that she would have preferred sawing both of her feet off, rather than wearing these shoes. SHE

48

HATED THEM. As she wiggled her big toe upon command, my dad said, "Okay great," and with that, grabbed both pairs of shoes and marched toward the register. My sister and I walked together in silence and rode home in the same manner. I tried to like the shoes. I took them in the house, tried them on with a few things and, eventually, I felt I could make them work, but I knew in the depths of my soul that these shoes had been made for an 88-year-old man who could either no longer tie his shoes, or quite frankly didn't care to. These were the shoes handed out at Shady Pines Nursing Home to new occupants; they were a standard part of the uniform. Yet, here we were, ages ten and twelve, strapped and ready to roll.

As I wrapped up my extravagant Christmas list, everyone, including Felicia, applauded me with their smiles before we moved to the main gym floor for a class dodge ball game. No one had to know I was different. No one had to know I wasn't like them. This way, I was part of the crowd; they accepted me. I remember this as one of the first instances I felt insecure. It was also one of the first times I'd utilized ineffective methods to suppress my insecurity. By the time I was in my thirties, I'd established a wide array of options meant to suppress my insecurities, depending on the situation. That's the thing about insecurity, the longer it's with you, the better you become at denying or pacifying its existence.

Journal Moment

Can you think of any ways you have supplemented your insecurity? Think of known insecurities you have. Now think about how you feel when they surface. What is the first thing you do? How do you function until the feelings subside? Be thorough and open with yourself in describing how you feel and how you cope.

SIGN & SYMPTOMS

"The older you get, the more you understand how your conscience works. The biggest and only critic lives in your perception of people's perception of you rather than people's perception of you." - Criss Jami

As stated before, the presence of characteristic insecurity is both negative and harmful. When housed, it may appear dormant and inactive but, in most cases, is a very powerful commander for much of what we desire and pursue, as well as how we function. Like any other abnormality, it will produce signs and symptoms of its activity. Since your mental structure is the first thing insecurity directly attacks, it then has access to your emotions. It is a large part of our human make-up to respond to our emotions with action. There are many signs that reveal the operation of insecurity—some are listed below.

<u>Symptoms of Insecurity:</u>
*Fear
*Anxiety
*Emotional Unrest
*Envy
*Jealousy
*Constant Comparison
*Cynicism
*Distrust
*Manipulation
*Control
*Pride
*Vanity & Snobbery
*Bragging & Habitual Self-Praise
*Arrogance
*Defensiveness
*Offensiveness
*Self-Loathing
*Self-Righteousness
*Selfishness
*Anger
*Stubbornness
*Rebellion

*Lying
*Aggression

When insecurity operates in our lives, it usually attaches itself to most of our emotions; however, it tends to show forth in certain emotions more than others. It does this as we utilize coping mechanisms during our moments of discomfort, rather than dealing directly with the issue. The coping mechanisms enable us to live with insecurity as we continue to pacify it. It's like the aspirin we take for a recurring toothache, instead of getting the tooth pulled. The cycle is endless as we learn to cope with the debilitating presence of insecurity by finding ways to divert or suppress it. Coping mechanisms become a large part one's personality. These mechanisms also cause people who are not discerning or able to see beneath the surface, to quickly label a person according to them, because they are often the most explicit characteristics. Also, since coping mechanisms are frequently what we use to conceal our insecurities, they can be deceivingly appealing to the uninformed, causing us to be celebrated for them. However, for us, they provide an escape from the discomfort of living with the unstable feelings we have toward ourselves, especially when we have employed these mechanisms for as long as we have been alive.

PERSONALITY TRAITS & COPING MECHANISMS

"Most bad behavior comes from insecurity." - Deborah Winger

Here are some of the personality traits, or qualities that are often present when insecurity is in operation. Pay close attention, and be willing to admit if you perhaps see yourself in any of these.

THE CONTROL FREAK

"Imperfect preparation gives rise to the thousand-fold forms that express physical and mental inferiority and insecurity."
- Alfred Adler

The desire for control is not the result of pride, as much as it is fear of what happens without it. A "control freak" is someone who seeks to have control in most situations they are involved in, especially those that directly affect their lives or the lives of those they are attached to. Until they have control, they are restless and agitated. In advanced cases, control freaks will stop at nothing until they obtain the result(s) they want, even if it means overstepping boundaries, interfering in decision-making, and providing feedback or suggestions beyond what is asked of them. If control is not granted to them, they erect walls of anger, spite, vengeance, and manipulation, making them difficult to get along with. If necessary, control freaks will take on the victim role to gain sympathy and to shame others in an effort to gain control. Without control they are critical, fault-finding, and judgmental of any other process or result that comes into manifestation apart from their control. Their fear produces a logic that convinces them that the more control they have, the better chance they have of controlling the outcome and lessening odds of harm, loss, or danger.

THE INTROVERT

"It's not all bad. Heightened self-consciousness, apartness, an inability to join in, physical shame and self-loathing—they are not all bad. Those devils have been my angels. Without them I would never have disappeared into language, literature, the mind, laughter and all the mad intensities that made and unmade me." - Stephen Fry

Some people are naturally introvert, as they typically enjoy the peace and solitude found alone or in the company of very few people, as opposed to a crowd. There are also people who are made introvert by the negative feelings and emotions associated with exposure to groups. The difference between the two types of introverts is the presence of self-love. A natural introvert has a healthy self-view and lives at peace, whereas an insecurity-induced introvert avoids others due to the lack of self-love and peace, making it difficult to interact with others without an internal struggle. When in groups, the fear of how they will be perceived or accepted becomes a point of anxiety and discomfort for the latter introvert. They struggle with conversation and interaction out of fear of saying or doing the wrong thing and being misunderstood. If they engage in conversation or interaction while in the presence of others, they often leave the gathering, and minutes, hours, days, and weeks after, struggle with anxiety pertaining to how they were perceived. Often mistaken for being shy and withdrawn, they sensor themselves to avoid scrutiny, but when with family or

52

friends, all of which they've found a place of acceptance, they are the polar opposite—fun and talkative. They feel it's easier to be alone because without people, there is no pressure to conform to the setting or contend with fear. It isn't that they enjoy their own company, it's that the discomfort they feel within themselves is a level of dysfunction they have come to understand and be able to better maintain while alone. It is the lesser of two evils. Their greatest fear is how they will be perceived or viewed by others.

THE COMPETITIVE

"The actual confident man, the man truly sure of himself, is not he who esteems himself higher than others, but he who is sure enough that he can bear to esteem others higher than himself." - Criss Jami

People who are naturally competitive, are driven by a challenge and desire to win; they experience a joy that comes from overcoming obstacles. In most cases, they are competing with themselves, pushing themselves, and working to be their best. If they lose, it does not become a factor in their opinion of themselves. They neither use the win or loss to determine their overall value, nor the value of anyone else. On the contrary, when someone's competitive nature is driven by insecurity, the win or loss becomes the measuring point of their own, as well as everyone else's worth. In the latter case, competitors become unspoken enemies or rivals. Those who operate out of insecurity, view competitors as threats to their reign, position, authority, and recognition. Failure to be recognized as the best, causes the insecure competitor to feel overlooked and/or inferior. They struggle to give compliments, recommendations, or praises to others, because of the overwhelming feeling that in doing so, their own worth is somehow diminished. However, they don't mind benefiting people who are not perceived threats to what they've established. Prone to jealousy and envy, these types of competitors employ other methods such as negative conversations, sowing discord, spreading rumors, and rejoicing in the downfall of others, in an attempt to, themselves, be seen in a more positive light. Good news about someone else's promotion, is not always good news to the insecure competitor. The greatest fear of the insecure competitor is the loss of respect and admiration from others.

THE COMPARER

"The reason that we struggle with insecurity, is because we compare our "behind the scenes" to everyone else's highlight reel."
– Pastor Steven Furtick

People who constantly compare themselves to others, are those who are working to secure solid opinions of themselves. When an individual is not sure of who they are, they use the lives and patterns of others as a measuring tool for who they should be. Following the example of those they believe are most praised, adored, recognized, and accomplished, the "comparer" uses them as a goal for where they should be, and a realization of where they are not. In turn, comparing their lives to others helps them decide their own value or lack thereof. By looking at someone else, they make assessments as to whether or not they are too fat or too skinny, successful or unsuccessful, adequate or inadequate. Susceptible to emulating and copying, those who constantly compare themselves to others are reflections of their influences, rarely establishing or appreciating what makes them unique. If they determine they have exceeded the accomplishments of those they admire, they celebrate themselves. If they determine they have fallen short of the accomplishment of those they admire, they ridicule themselves. Their greatest fear is never achieving for themselves, what they admire about others.

THE NARCISSIST (PROUD & ARROGANT)

"Insecurity attracts two conditions: pride and identity. Pride will mask insecurity, whereas identity heals it."
- Gayle Brannan

Narcissism is often mistaken for pride and arrogance, and sometimes even masked as self-confidence and strength. Yet, in reality, the narcissist has come to be who they are as the result of deep insecurity concealed through various methods. Bragging, putting others down, adopting prejudices, and anything that adds to and serves to build their opinion of themselves, is how they survive. Often inclined to self-praise and compliment fishing, narcissists desire constant affirmation to mask negative feelings about themselves. To escape low self-esteem and insecurity, they self-medicate through selfish means. Prone to compulsiveness and addictive personalities, they often settle on supplementing through gambling, alcoholism, drugs, or sexual promiscuity, in advanced cases. Unteachable, dogmatic, and unable to accept help, information, or teaching from others, narcissists trust their word and direction above all others. Their deep need for recognition drives them to be their own biggest fans, and most social cues that are naturally formed in other people over time, are not developed or utilized in narcissistic individuals, as such cues aren't necessary in a world that only revolves around them. Known to be irrational, stubborn, offensive, rebellious, and easily offended, narcissists rarely apologize, as it is difficult to get them to see their wrongs, and even harder for them to admit them. If and when they do admit they're wrong, the vulnerability causes them a great deal of discomfort. Humility is an assumed quality, but is only seen when forced; when this happens, narcissists view it as more of a weakness than a strength. They often take on the role of a rebel, constantly needing a cause to fight. Narcissists believe that conformity, even to what is right, takes away their ability to be viewed as unique and valuable. Always the leader, and rarely a follower, they will sacrifice their own well-being before they submit to another, resulting from their trust issues. Their greatest fear is that their weaknesses and vulnerability will be exposed.

THE PEOPLE-PLEASER

"People's approval and acceptance is a false cure for insecurity. While believing that it's cured because the symptom disappears, it actually becomes the poison that feeds it, giving it further life and strength."
- Shaunee Brannan

The "people-pleaser" is someone who's ability to say "yes" or "no" is not determined by what they want to do, but what someone else wants them to do—something they believe will gain them approval or acceptance. Using their own time and resources as tools, they work and give what they have to others, even when they shouldn't, hoping to be accepted as the result. They will re-arrange their schedules, shuffle duties, or even place those who already love and accept them last in line, to serve the needs of those whose acceptance they are working to gain. Always second-guessing themselves and easily persuaded, they typically utilize many influences to determine the course of their own lives. Sometimes mistaken for being selfless or generous, people-pleasers are often preyed on by sociopath's and selfish individuals. However, what is viewed as selfless and dependable, is really a deep desire to be accepted. Their fear is rejection or exposure to things they view as inadequacies.

THE OVERACHIEVER

"Being Overconfident often exists when one tries to cover up one's insecurities without facing them." - Edmond Mbiaka

Overachievers are usually labeled as ambitious, driven, and focused, all of which are typically true of them. Yet, these qualities are produced as a result of the way(s) they supplement their insecurities. Working tirelessly, overachievers believe success through their careers, family life, positions, and even extra-curricular activities, are the things that eliminate their inadequacies. It usually doesn't just stop with them. The choice of mates, friendships, and even their children and the direction of their lives, become "feats" added to their list of accomplishments. Overachievers tend to give their all in everything they do, believing their effort eliminates the possibility of failure. They are not as driven by a desire for the future, as they are by the past they hope to never to return to. Prone to pride and snobbery, they use their accomplishments to categorize their worth and the worth of others, and often only give respect and/or time to those they feel are an asset to them. For an overachiever, failure and loss are met by depression and feelings of anxiety, as they fear the possible outcomes of failure.

THE CONSTANT COMIC

"I did not want to appear before the world as pathetic, depressed, and psychologically ill. So I erected a barrier of words and wit around myself, so that nobody could see how needy I really was." - Karen Armstrong

Often viewed as the "life of the party," or the "fun one" in the group, the "constant comic" is, in all actuality, very uncomfortable in their own skin. They are often people who struggle with depression, low self-esteem, and self-loathing. They have searched themselves and struggle to find qualities that make them feel valuable, aside from their humor. Using both humor and constant talking to suppress and deflect attention from their insecurities, it is their goal to keep people, themselves included, from seeing the turmoil inside of them and to, instead, help them feel more accepted. Moments of intimacy and seriousness tend to make them uncomfortable, as they struggle to connect. When these moments present themselves, causing suppressed emotions to rise, the comic will either joke or laugh the moment away, in an effort to relieve the tension associated with feeling undesired emotions. Evading these emotions often causes one to become numb, callous, disconnected, and to behave inappropriately during times that require focus, compassion, or spirituality. The comic's fear is dealing with suppressed memories and emotions that reveal their internal view of themselves.

THE HATER, GOSSIP, & FAULT-FINDER

"Insecurity is an ugly thing. It makes you hate people that you don't even know." - Unknown

These types of people have found their own lives to be uneventful, full of failure, or something they would rather not face, and have given up on repairing what's broken. They might have also been wounded by life's events and never received the healing necessary to live a balanced life. They are typically unaware that their wounds are the seeds of their insecurity. They are usually so busy looking at others, that they become prisoners of denial. Through insecurity, they supplement by tearing others down. Their success is based on the failures of others. Talking about others is the easiest way to distract themselves and those around them from seeing their faults. Usually a member of a clique or circle of people that mirror their own conditions, they build relationships based on negative commonalities, and all members of the clique feed off one another for validity, importance, and strength. The ability to stand alone is non-existent. It is difficult to give credit where it's due because it puts them in a deficit, as it goes against their method of gaining from the losses of others. Loss, failure, downfall, and bad news for others, becomes good news for them. They don't typically discuss other people's good news, except when they are working to hide their true intentions and motives. When given the opportunity, they plant seeds of negativity, in an effort to weaken what is positive. Through cynicism, sarcasm, and over-analyzing, they often find the negative in positive things. For what they don't know, they use assumptions, probability, and theory, to fill in the blanks. It is not that they have an inability to see the good in others—their issue lies in how they feel when they see it, especially when it's celebrated or appreciated by others, because it forces them to reflect on their own condition or progress. They gain acceptance by being the first to have "the scoop," and the first to tell it. By using constant conversation as a diversion, their hope is to keep people from seeing their own issues and faults—the things that they like least about themselves. Ultimately, their greatest fear is facing themselves.

THE SELF-RIGHTEOUS

"For the believer, humility is honesty about one's greatest flaws to a degree in which he is fearless about truly appearing less righteous than another."
- Criss Jami

For those who choose to supplement their insecurities with thoughts of self-righteousness, it's like investing a million dollars into building a mansion made out of cards. If and when the self-righteous fails, their entire world crumbles, due to the beliefs they have established about themselves and others. Self-righteous thoughts are only possible by those who have been shaped by doctrine, moral standards, or laws, in order to have a mark of acceptance or something to overcome. It's usually the people who have either escaped a life of immorality or been exposed to legalism that opposes it, shaping their thoughts that failure, on a moral and practical level, is one of the worst human flaws—worthy of shame. Since they have arrived at a place where they believe they are free from failure, they use a platform of subconscious perfection to criticize others. In actuality, they are not people who are unaware of their issues, it's actually the reverse. Many of them have deep internal struggles with resolving past issues, or battle immoral thoughts and feelings, causing them to feel insecure, unworthy, and ashamed. Without the proper resolve of these thoughts, the self-righteous carry insecurities they choose to satisfy through a judgement-based approach that makes them, by their "good"

58

behavior, superior to others. Since the mark of perfection is very narrow and impossible to reach, appearing perfect leads the self-righteous to believe they're better than most. They use self-righteous thoughts to fight the fear of inadequacy and underachieving.

THE VAIN & MATERIALISTIC

"It is common knowledge among psychologists that most of us underrate ourselves, short-change ourselves, sell ourselves short. Actually, there is no such thing as a superiority complex. People who seem to have one are actually suffering from feelings of inferiority; their "superior" self is a fiction, a cover-up, to hide from themselves and others their deep-down feelings of inferiority and insecurity." - Maxwell Maltz

Much of society ascribes to the belief that "the more you have, the more you are." People who choose to supplement their insecurities through vanity and materialism are those working to escape a lesser view of themselves. It is usually employed by those who struggle with grasping a natural, positive, internal self-image that doesn't require additions. It can be found operating in polar opposites, but is the result of the same condition. The woman who was repeatedly called ugly by classmates as a child, or the woman who has been told she's beautiful her entire life, differ in that one believes vanity is the answer to inadequacy, while the other believes she's adequate because she's beautiful. However, they are both similar in that they have used something trivial, circumstantial, and fleeting, to satisfy an eternal quality. It is also a typical trait of those born into low-income homes or into wealth. For those who grew up in lack, they work to overcome feelings of inadequacy by adding things, often material, to themselves to gain the respect of others. For those who were born into prosperity, without the right guidance, or with guardians who have used the same method to supplement their own insecurity, these type of people become shaped by the idea that "they are what they have." They will go great lengths to perfect flaws that are visible to others, sometimes using a facade, illegal methods, and dishonesty, to support a false public persona. Image and appearance are very important to them. In order to determine their worth and to shape their reputation, they judge both themselves and others using their status and material possessions. Their greatest fears include the loss of adoration, wealth, and status.

THE DECEITFUL & THE LIAR

"The truly scary thing about undiscovered lies is that they have a greater capacity to diminish us than exposed ones. They erode our strength, our self-esteem, our very foundation." - Cheryl Hughes

Truth is only appreciated by those who believe in its freedom. People who operate in deception are people who are afraid of the results truth will bring. In an effort to feel secure, they build up walls of deception to support and cover themselves from loss, harm, rejection, consequence, and exposure. Being the victim of a liar or deceiver can elicit feelings of anger, resentment, strife, and sorrow, but the accused are most frequently the people who actually need the greatest amount compassion. Most of them have adopted the habit of lying to deal with pain stemming from an earlier point in their lives, leaving them with deep-rooted insecurity and fear. In the eyes of a liar, deceiving provides safety and acceptance, as it gives them a believed state of control over being harmed again. Often pathological in nature, they lie to the point of either believing themselves or forgetting their lies. They are not completely opposed to the truth, but only when the truth benefits or supports the result(s) they are pursuing, will they operate in it. For those whose fear and insecurity have led them down paths where self-control is lacking, they act out in ways that harvest shame and regret. It becomes easier to lie about their behavior, rather than change the coping methods that they use to numb their pain. Above all, deceivers and liars fear the perceived consequences of truth.

THE VIOLENT & THE TOUGH GUY

"The hallmark of insecurity is bravado." - Brandon Sanderson

People who succumb to violent behavior to settle matters, are not typically looking to settle matters at all, but to release feelings for which they have no resolve. It is often not the target of their violence that has driven them to strike, but feelings of helplessness, having unanswered questions, and a level of discomfort caused by vulnerability they feel they cannot manage. The true opponent is never who they are fighting externally, but what they are fighting internally. They are on a continuous quest to redeem themselves, to themselves.

60

Deep within, they carry a victim's mentality, having suffered under abuse of power, abuse of authority, manipulation, control, bullying, sexual, verbal and/or emotional abuse, rejection, or being underestimated, thus causing them deep-rooted anger, as they often think, I will never let that happen to me again. The desire to fight or prove they are not pushovers is an effort to overcome feelings of inadequacy that result from being mistreated at some point, or failure to be able to defend themselves against others. As the result of their insecurity, they will face a lion, a speeding train, or a man or woman three times their size, without backing down. The fear they host is based on inadequacy, shame, and weakness, all of which result from failure to defend or be defended.

THE RACIST & PREJUDICE

I'm interested in the fact that the less secure a man is, the more likely he is to have extreme prejudice." - Clint Eastwood

The internal quality of adopting segregation, oppression, categorizing, elimination, and discrimination against others based on stereotypical beliefs, gender, race, ability, disability, appearance, education, economic status, religion, among other things, is only made possible through the presence of insecurity. Such characteristics symbolize extreme weakness used by people to establish value and superiority. The idea is that in order to be the best, someone else must be the worst. Racism and prejudice that is blatant and overt is no different than that which is hidden. They each serve the purpose of supplementing a great insecurity that says, "I am not good enough." For this, I give compassion.

CAN YOU BE HONEST?

Has any/all of this made you a little uncomfortable? Did you squirm? Did you see yourself in here at any point? What about your co-worker, best friend, spouse, child, or anyone else you know? Either you said, "Aha! That explains it?" Or maybe you sat in silence because it hit too close to home. Maybe you think I need to shut my raging pie hole. Maybe you're saying to yourself, "she's no Ph.D., or nothin' close! How does she know any of this?" You're wrong. I **Personally**

Hosted **D**eficiency for 30+ years. I have a certificate and degree in Insecurity. I have pulled from and employed every last personality trait listed above, at some point in my life, as I struggled with insecurity and a lack of identity. I am not telling you anything I haven't, myself, dealt with. Things are getting more personal for both you and me, because we're getting to the root of the issue. Let's discover where it all began.

Journal Moment

Consider all the emotions and different personality traits listed. Did you see yourself in any of them? If so, which ones? Has any of this helped you better understand certain relationships in your life? Write down everything you're thinking and feeling, especially feelings and memories that have been exposed as the result of what you've read.

5

MAN vs. WOMAN

"No temptation has overtaken you except what is common to mankind. And God is faithful; he will not let you be tempted beyond what you can bear. But when you are tempted, he will also provide a way out so that you can endure it."
- 1 Corinthians 10:13, NIV

I remember reading a blog post about a woman who described her issues with self-confidence, after years of struggling with her weight. She detailed her angst and constant struggle to like herself. Several comments in response to the post, were from people encouraging her and connecting with her struggle. Then I noticed two or three comments that in so many words said, "Yeah, I know what you mean. Men don't have to deal with this!" Oh, I beg to differ! After dating over the years, living with a father, two brothers, a husband, and being a pastor to men, I've found that they, too, carry insecurities, some that are similar to those women carry. I stated early in the book that insecurity is not gender based. It is a characteristic given to humanity, and will attach to anyone unequipped to deal with it.

There is, however, a difference in how men and women express or deal with their insecurities. Each individual is different and adopts their own coping mechanisms to endure it. But, according to the way God created us, there are some ways that are common amongst men and women. For those of you who may be struggling in relationships with a spouse, a love interest, your children, a family member, a co-worker, or others, you may be misdiagnosing the issue by not considering the insecurity driving it. It can often be hard to see insecurity for what it is, since most of our external experiences typically disguise it as something else, resulting from the mechanisms we utilize to cover it.

This is a very critical chapter for people in relationships, or those on the road to marriage. Let me tell you something, it is very dangerous to date, build friendships, or get married, with insecurity ruling you. Relationships are typically the main ways we seek to supplement our insecurity. Feeling unloved and unaccepted often cause our insecurities to come into existence or to be strengthened. One of the first things we do to satisfy such feelings is search for someone who we believe will fill the void. The maintenance required to do this is exhausting, especially when we choose to entertain someone who mirrors our own conditions. It is one of the most superficial ways to feel better, but not to be better. As a matter of fact, we end up adding to the damage already caused by our insecurities. If you are even a little bit aware that you still have a lot of work to do in this area, hold off on finding someone. Stop the search. Close down the dating app for a minute. Tell him to stop calling you for a little while. Tell her you're taking some time to yourself. Turn down a few dates, and don't accept the proposal just yet. Wait until you're healed and whole. Once that happens, you just might look up and ask, "Who are you? And why are we dating again?" Take my advice. You'll thank me later.

HE SAID

"A man's spirit is free, but his pride binds him with chains of suffocation in a prison of his own insecurities"
- Jeremy Aldana

If I had ever thought men didn't experience insecurity, the thought would have been demolished when, as a newlywed, I was able to get a front row seat to the process of a young, handsome man, losing his hair. We were 30 years old and my husband, Gayle, was still as handsome and youthful as when we'd first met. Not that he isn't still smoking hot, but he was sizzling hot then. Within the second year of our marriage, he started experiencing thinning of his rich, blonde locks. He'd always worn his hair fairly short, but his visits to the barber started confirming that his follicular erosion was soon to come. At first he was in denial. He'd say, "Boy, I gotta stop wearing those hats! They're jacking up my hair! But it'll grow back, give it a week or two. My hair grows fast." But when those couple of weeks finally rolled around, there was more hair missing and he started making less hopeful confessions about the comeback of his bangs. Being the realist I am, I would frankly say, "Um...no, Sugar Crumb. That's called genetics. The Lord giveth, and the Lord taketh away. He's asking for His hairs back." He'd say, "But my dad still has a head full of hair!" He was adamant about his hair growing back until one day, I heard him sneaking and calling his mother. "Mom, how did your father look?

Did he have hair?" He asked. I could barely hear her voice through the phone, but coupled with his expression, and me making out the words "bald" and "thinning" somewhere in her response, I knew it was finally sinking in that, in the future, he would only be going to the barber to have his mustache and beard trimmed. Realizing there was a problem, he started trying a few different hair loss products. It started with the shampoo and topical treatment serum, but those hairs of his were still putting up a fight. Then, one day I walked in the house to see Gayle and another gentleman who had recently suffered from hair loss. They were sitting on the couch, facing the TV, quiet as church mice. I walked in and said my "hello's" while looking at the mail; I never really looked directly at the two of them. Once I finally glanced up from the stack of mail in my hands I asked "What on earth is that smell?" I noticed they both had a 6-inch tall pile of white foam on the tops of their heads. I stood still for a minute. They were both quiet, using their peripheral vision to see if I was looking at them. I think they'd each hoped I wouldn't get home before their hair— well, the hair they still had left on their heads, finished marinating.

"Lord Jesus, Holy Father of the planets and beyond. What are you guys doing?!" I asked them. They burst out laughing, mouths wide open. They'd gone out on a limb and bought a $50 box of what they thought was the next big thing. It promised to restore hair growth but, not to my surprise, it didn't work. It took a little while for reality to sink in, but one day after I called my husband "Mr. Belding" from *Saved by The Bell,* he finally decided to get rid of the remaining hair on the sides and back of his head. It took a while, but he finally settled into his new look and built the confidence necessary to accept that, with age, he was changing. It was a vulnerable time for him, but it gave me the opportunity to see a side of him that most men wouldn't dare let anyone see.

Men's insecurities are based on the same factors that apply to women: what they believe about God and themselves. There are many men who have been exposed to damaging conditions, just as women have. Abuse, rejection, affirmation, and their upbringings, all aid in shaping the way men see themselves. Also, society has played a great role in shaping how we view men and what we expect of them. Society has caused many to believe that a man should be strong, in charge of himself and his family, and a leader in the community. Any sign of emotional awareness such as crying, compassion, or kindness, can be viewed as a weakness or a measuring tool of his manliness. This is often difficult for men who have been raised by a single mother or with sisters, and no predominant male influence. They often take on feminine qualities, having been exposed to and shaped by them in their early years. Sometimes these qualities are used to determine the sexual orientation of a man. Whether or not it delivers accurate results, it is an unfair measuring tool, because if men fall short of what is expected of them, the way they see themselves is also negatively impacted. Based on societal beliefs, some men work to build facades or utilize supplements that, at the very least, cause them to look the part, until they can achieve the part.

In general, men are far less expressive communicators than women. If you ask both a man and a woman to give an account of an event, the man's account will likely be shorter and include far less details. On the contrary, the woman is more likely to fill in all the blanks, adding colorful details, as well as her opinion, when she deems necessary. In addition to communicating less expressively, because of how society has shaped how we view men, when there are weaknesses or struggles, men are far more prone to conceal them. For men, concealing things becomes a way to survive certain conditions. In their minds, they nurse the thought, *I can change when I'm ready*. Men may also believe that they have their issues under control. It often takes several mistakes, some irreversible, for men to admit that there may be a bigger issue than they'd hoped. Many times, these issues are not confronted until people, men and women, are married. Having a spouses often causes us to confront the problems our spouses may also be confronting. When my husband and I got married, every last thing we had suppressed came to the surface. You don't realize how selfish, petty, and carnal you are, or the depths of your strengths and weaknesses, until you get married. When Gayle and I were dating, I'd get mad at him and dump him every other month. Once we were married, the dumping trick didn't work anymore. There were significant issues to be worked out between us. I was the catalyst by which God used to tell Gayle, "You can't run from this anymore. Deal with it," and vice versa. This is partially why a lot of men don't want to get married. Sometimes the accountability a partner represents is viewed negatively by those who have supplemented to the point that they prefer dysfunction over change.

Though men and women struggle with many of the same insecurities, our methods and choices of supplements sometimes differ. Often, the supplements men choose counteractive images that are the direct opposite of how they are perceived. The belief is that it will help others view them as the opposite of how they are currently viewed. If perceived as weak, a man might choose to supplement in a way that causes him to exhibit "bully" and "tough guy" characteristics. If it is assumed that a man is confused about his sexual orientation, he might entertain a plethora of women and have multiple sex partners to dispel such assumptions. Insecurities regarding a man's appearance are met with vigorous gym workouts, vain behavior, and playboy activities, in order to compliment him and build his confidence until he no longer feels unwanted. Some men may also have male friendships that mirror where they are, instead of where they would like to be. You can tell a lot about a man by the company he keeps. None of us, male or female, build friendships that are not reflections of who we are, or who we once were.

Men are typically trophy-oriented—all about the win and bragging rights. This is not their faults; I believe it's the way God made men, but that they have been further shaped by society, dating back to the beginning of time, where brute and strength equaled respect. Competition is very much a part of what men enjoy. The problem with this is that a man with an unhealthy self-image uses this innate quality to build competition in areas it doesn't belong. I have seen this insecurity surface in politics, religion, and even in the family. For the man who insecure about his image, he may consider choosing a spouse as a quest to find a trophy wife. The better she looks, the better he looks, and the more he's respected. The idea is, if she's with him, there must be something about him that's special. Now let's be clear, regardless of whether or not they are insecure, most men love beautiful things. I don't care who they are, men, no matter their sexual preference, notice pretty women. There's a reason why homosexual men often love having women as their best friends and adore the beauteous side of women. Despite a man's sexual preference, he will always innately appreciate the beauty of a woman. God made men visually inclined. They are usually attracted visually before they are mentally. When they are working to fix insecurities by using status, their selection of a spouse is based on what will aid them in their image. I have witnessed many men bypass women who may not have been as physically attractive, but who were everything else they needed and desired, for women who were beautiful on the outside, but lacked the internal and enduring qualities that mattered most. I have also seen men settle for women they knew they didn't love, but who they believed would be resources for them in life. Not only is this a selfish tendency, but a sign of extreme insecurity. Again, only insecurity causes us to use people as supplements, especially by pre-meditation. It takes a very secure and well-informed man to consider and choose what is most important.

SHE SAID

"I was never weighed down by beauty in my lifetime. However, I was beaten down by the sad fears of my gender- women who didn't allow you to feel pretty or rejoice in who you are, unless it fell beneath how they thought about themselves."

- Shannon L. Adler

Women are a lot less willing and able to cover insecurities, as we are naturally more communicative and emotional. We are more likely to express our feelings and emotions, thus revealing our concerns, whether or not they are valid. However, like men, we also succumb to competition, at times; yet, our motives and intentions are birthed from a different place. It seems that friction has always been high among women. I've seen this to be true from an early age, especially as it pertains to behaviors fueled by jealousy. I used to wonder where it began, but after reading many bible stories, I can tell you it started at the very beginning of time. In the Old Testament, men were encouraged to have multiple wives. Wives and concubines were considered commodities—signs of wealth and power. The more wives a man had, the more children, desirably sons, he would have, which led to more respect in society. The problem was, one man with 15 wives and 100 children, meant a lot of pressure on the women to exceed their competition, in an effort to receive attention and favor. This behavior has carried on to our present time. To this day, many women are still at odds over men, but also over any and everything else. The truth in all this is that women who are jealous and competitive, are actually at war with themselves.

As women, a great amount of our insecurities stem from our appearance. I don't know a woman who isn't working on something

68

externally concerning herself. Many of us are convinced we need to lose a pound or two, or fix "this" and "that." Overall, we are very critical and sometimes unforgiving of ourselves. So many of us have allowed our self-images to be shaped by the media. This issue with this is that the media often portrays us in a way that highlights sexual contributions as a major determinant of our worth. Most women are mentally working to either discredit these portrayals or live up to them. To define our own beauty and worth, we typically use tools that have already been accepted or considered suitable to make such determinations. What I mean is, popular television characters, pop icons, and those who seem to have the attention and adoration of men, are usually the women we long to imitate, even if their internal composition is dysfunctional. It is not *them* we admire; it is the attention they receive. As women, we are guilty of supplementing by comparison. Using what has been established by "them," (don't you hate when people say "they" and nobody knows who "they" are?) we compare ourselves. Comparing puts us at an immediate disadvantage.

Even if by comparison you find yourself at the top, you have really only managed to feed your insecurity with something that is superficial and inaccurate. Often, our comparisons are made up of only part of the truth about who we're comparing ourselves to. In order to accurately compare yourself to another person, you need every last detail of who they are, to make a complete and fair analysis. Ladies and gentlemen, please hear me now: the only people we should ever compare ourselves to in an effort to gauge our progress, is ourselves and God. Using God as our measuring tool, we have a foundation of how to operate in life. With such a tool, we are able to compare ourselves to ourselves, at different stages and seasons of our lives. Shaunee at age 18, shouldn't have looked like Shaunee at age 25. I should be able to sit and compare who I was then, to who I am now, noting how I have changed. Comparing yourself to yourself is the fairest and most effective way to change you. You are your *only* competition.

In addition to outer appearances, as women, we suffer insecurities birthed through toxic and failed relationships. When a woman is rejected by a man whose affection she's seeking, it becomes another moment to live down, especially if she has invested anything she deems valuable (money, sex, time) into the relationship. If by some chance the man moves on quickly, like most do, she is left comparing herself to his new love interest. Even if 9 out of 10 of her qualities measure up to the new interest, the one that doesn't, becomes the one that grabs ahold of her mind and causes her to think less of herself. I have witnessed many women choose men who were financially well-off or appeared to be stable, all because they were not well-off financially and lacked stability of their own. Instead of working to be self-sufficient, these types of women are usually unmotivated as a result of the negative influences of insecurity. What I mean is, it is typically not an issue of laziness or complacency, but the belief that they will be unsuccessful at securing a future for themselves. For this reason, the search then turns to someone who already has what they perceive as a future. Absent of love, relationships like this never work out. You cannot use artificial things to satisfy eternal needs.

As women, when we surround ourselves with other women who struggle with insecurity, the nature of the conversation will reflect the struggle. Unstable relationships are built on insecurity. Meaningful relationships are built on security. When there is a group of women who are unsure of who they are, they pull from one another to establish themselves as a clique. If someone decides to leave the clique and go in search of their identity, whichever element they added to the group that helped uphold its image, also leaves. A clique's power lies in their numbers. When a woman is secure, her friendships reflect who she is and where she's going. In meaningful relationships, negative conversation and gossip do not serve as the glue that holds relationships together, nor does excluding others help establish superiority. Meaningful relationships are built on trust and a genuine desire to see others succeed, even if such success doesn't directly benefit you.

Without trying, I have always stood out. This is part of my God-given DNA. By nature, I have always been a leader, even during the most insecure moments of my life. I have always been able to persuade and encourage people in a certain direction. As I began coming into an understanding of God's love for me, my ability to guide people in the right direction increased, and so did the amount of women who didn't like me because of it. I would constantly come in contact with women who were insecure. There was a time when I realized that even women in the church struggled with deep-rooted insecurity. They'd gather in groups and talk about me, or work to sabotage my efforts. I remember being 19 years old. A woman who was 15 years older than me came up to me and said, "I just want to apologize to you. I've hated you for a whole year. Then God showed me that I was jealous of you!" I had some inkling that I'd perhaps, occasionally, got on her nerves, having caught her sucking her lips and rolling her eyes at me a few times. Still, to hear her say she'd held hatred against me, baffled me. I stood there, dumbfounded, looking at her. I wish she would have used wisdom in telling me the truth, but, nonetheless, it was an eye-opener. Then, there were three women at my job, the eldest being 20 years my senior, who huddled together in an attempt to get me fired. After two write-ups and being on my way to the third and final, I went to God and asked for help, because two of the three woman worked in the Human Resources department, so I felt the odds were stacked against me. Within a week after I'd first gone to God in prayer, the head honcho of the three was demoted, another had her position eliminated, and the last began sucking up to me so bad that I almost bought her a pacifier. All of this happened out of the blue, so they thought. The truth is, God really had me covered. He wasn't going to let jealousy-fueled intentions ruin where He'd positioned me. Yet, in everything that had happened, I still had such compassion for them; it was a natural part of me. I didn't wish them even a little bit of the harm they'd wished me.

Women would take one look at me, how I was dressed, the men who pursued me, and the accomplishments I'd made, and determine that I thought I was "all that." They didn't know how badly I wanted to believe I was "all that." I represented who some women wanted to be, and if they ever got there, THEY would "Think I'M all that." So I ended up being labeled "guilty as charged," by someone else's admission! I was often perceived to be someone I wasn't because of standards these women had created for me, without really knowing me. For quite some time, I would go around women who were intimidated by me, and the fact that they couldn't even look me in the eye and have a conversation, made me uncomfortable. So, in my own insecurity, I worked hard to gain acceptance and show these women how down to earth I was. Sometimes I would resort to very silly, un-lady-like behavior, in order to connect with them. I was often quiet about my accomplishments and the good things that happened to me, because I was afraid to cause jealousy and/or envy. Being strong and confident by nature, it was very difficult misrepresenting who I naturally was, just to appeal to people who didn't know who they were.

After I came into real acceptance and identity through God, my desperate need to relate to people, subsided. Don't get me wrong, I still have certain flaws, but because of what I've experienced and how I've overcome what I have, I've become very good at spotting women who don't like other women simply because they don't like *themselves*. I always hug their necks the hardest, knowing that eventually they'll figure it out and, if necessary, I'm willing to be the sacrificial lamb in the interim. What I mean is, if I have to be the target by which they negatively satisfy their insecurities until they figure out that is just what they're doing, I'm willing to do so. After all, someone else did it for me. As I changed, my perspective did as well. Other women became less of a focus as self-awareness became more of a focus.

Women, take it from me. No matter how much you gossip about another woman, refuse to give her compliments, desire to see her fail, or position yourself above her, you must know this: Another person's failure does not make you successful. If you need someone to fail in order for you to feel better about yourself, you are insecure. Our feelings of envy and jealousy typically outlast the momentary joy that people, who our insecurities are geared toward, feel based on success. They walk away, go home to take their dress and makeup off, go to bed, and wake up the next morning, on to the next venture. Meanwhile, you walk away, rooted deeper in your insecurity, and two weeks later, you're still bothered by their "this" or "that," or that they have "this" or "that." The notion that "the way to the top is by pulling someone else down," further reveals why people who live by this, are where they are. It takes security to celebrate another person. If you cannot do it without a struggle, it's a sign that your aspirations are in the wrong place.

COMMONANILITIES

No matter what umbrella you fall under, there are some things that are true for everyone, and some that will always reveal the greatest influences on who we are as individuals. These influences are things that all of us will have to confront at some point. How we choose to do this may vary, but we all must resist the urge to supplement our insecurity. Our past and the ways we've processed them, cannot be ignored. Furthermore, without healing and reformation of our thinking, we will continue housing insecurities that damage our lives. Our maturity reveals our security. Immaturity is typically associated with children, as many of them are unable to process things using their life experiences, knowledge, and lessons. There is something about wisdom that experience provides—it teaches us and settle us. We start to learn who we are and who we are not, and as we learn who we aren't, wisdom helps further reveal who God is to us. We are as mature as we are secure.

Journal Moment

Consider your interactions with people. What are some ways you've witnessed male and female react to their insecurity? Can you think of someone you may have incorrectly labeled? Have you incorrectly labeled yourself?

Hi Insecurity. BYE Insecurity.

6

INSECURITY, WHEN DID YOU GET HERE?

"Love removes fear, in the same way fear then removes love. And the fruit of fear is insecurity." - Bishop Jamie Englehart

To understand how insecurity has affected your life, it is not enough to only know its definition and different forms. At the root of every insecurity is a belief. For most of us, the belief is a false one that has found root in our thinking. Discussing other things and never dealing with the origin of our insecurities, makes this a failed mission. If we are unable to pinpoint where and how our insecurities were birthed, we have also failed to uncover the lies that made them possible, and the things that are sustaining them. It is imperative that we reach deep within and go back to our earliest memories in life. This will be difficult for some of us to do, and may also be absolutely terrifying.

We often suppress painful and uncomfortable memories, in an effort to move beyond them. The problem here is that anything suppressed, is still *living*. Suppression doesn't necessarily equal inactivity. Even while suppressed, memories still have a way of influencing our subconscious mind, which impacts our feelings and actions. I am taking this moment to encourage you to grab ahold of courage and strength. This will be a time where both *circumstantial insecurity* and *characteristic insecurity* will surface. This is a time to push beyond the barriers intended to persuade you of your inability to make the necessary changes. Focus your mind and heart, and open yourself up to memories of your past. The walls of protection you've erected will have to come down. This is a moment that only you will experience. The defense mechanisms you typically use may try to manifest. Please don't use this time to dwell on where you are now, the career you've built for yourself, your marriage, goals, children, or any other successes. It's not the time to think about where you are or where you're going. Right now it's all about where you've been, because where you've already been, has a lot to do with where you are and where you're going. Hiding and covering up is not allowed, but I urge you to stand naked (figuratively speaking) and look at yourself in the mirror. If you cannot look yourself square in the eyes, you will never be able to look directly at insecurity and demand that it leave. If necessary, allow yourself to laugh or cry. It's okay to feel angry, happy, hurt, joyful, ashamed, embarrassed, silly, scared, defenseless, defensive, offensive, unattractive, attractive, or any other feeling that surfaces. As you journey into the past, it's okay to become in touch with past feelings, except blindness—DO NOT become blind. Don't let denial creep in, causing you to believe that what you're feeling isn't real. Don't let it convince you that your memories are false. I'm asking you to remember everything. In short, I am asking you to SEE. And as you see, prepare yourself for all that comes with it.

Please say this prayer with me:

Dear Lord, I am asking for Your help in this moment. Please help me to open my heart, mind, and reasoning to Your direction and leading. I make the commitment to let down my guards and walls for You to come in and reveal truth. I call forth every dormant memory. I ask that you reveal every deep-rooted lie in my heart. I receive the courage to face every fear and uncomfortable feeling. I open my heart and mind to change how I have settled these memories and allowed them to shape my life. I surrender my thinking. I surrender all my failures and victories, and I come as a child who knows nothing, but simply trusts. Please show me truth that will set me free. I embrace Your love for me, even if I don't yet know its truth or power. I ask that You make it a reality to me now. Walk with me as You open the eyes of my understanding. I will not lean to my own understanding. I am simply asking for Yours in this moment. I TRUST YOU.

Journal Moment

Pull from within. Allow this to be a sensitive and self-reflective moment. Write how you feel. If memories are already beginning to surface, write them down, along with the feelings they elicit. If memories have not yet started to surface, but you have feelings or emotions that have come as a result of your prayer, write those down, even if they are negative... especially if they are negative. Nothing is too miniscule or unimportant.

NOT GOOD ENOUGH FOR GOD

"What comes in our minds when we think about God is the most important thing about us." - A.W. Tozer

As I stated before, our insecurities reflect our beliefs concerning God and ourselves. We don't truly know how to view ourselves until we have established a view of God. Notice I didn't say this view of God has to be correct, it simply has to be one that is solidified in our thinking. If we decide there is no God, we turn to ourselves and humanity for direction and fulfillment in life. If we decide that Buddha is the one true God, we follow the teachings of Buddhism for our direction and fulfillment. If we decide that Jesus Christ is the one true God, we depend on His life, teachings, and the Bible, for our direction and fulfillment, so on and so forth. Our beliefs concerning God point to how we handle what has happened in our lives, and the things that lie at foundation of our insecurities.

This will probably be one of my most transparent and self-exposing chapters, even more than the later chapters that discuss the damages and regrets I suffered from my insecurities. Trust me, I have some doozies. Get your popcorn ready. This is the first time I will be publicly sharing details of my life that I have hardly ever voiced, let alone fully resolved, until I set out to write this book. And without a doubt, insecurity and intimidation tried rearing their heads. My desires to not be misunderstood and to not offend anyone, weighed heavy on me. However, I've realized there is no way around discussing how my own insecurities came to be, without being as transparent as possible. My prayer is that my heart is seen, and that I am able to use as much wisdom and tact as possible, without forsaking the truth. For those who may have been affected by the same conditions and have a completely different view, you're either very fortunate, or very much in denial. Yet, with much reflection and by praying the prayer above, I have come to see things differently.

Let me preface my story with this:

I understand that some things I say may be offensive and misunderstood by those who have experienced things similar to what I have, but have a different resolve. I also understand that the need to defend or rebuke may follow. Please know that if it were left up to me, I would have been happy to keep my lessons learned to myself, as I value peace above all else. Discussing topics like this usually result in a lack of peace by confrontation and intimidation. However, after prayer and deep reflection, I asked God to give me as much wisdom and tact as possible, to relay everything in a way that those who are not offended, are able to hear my heart and receive truth from what I am saying. I have no desire to attack a specific institution, religious structure, or belief system, nor to create conflict. I also have no ill-will or resentment in my heart, even though, after coming to the realization of how much of my life was affected by these things, I did at one time. My conclusions of life are much different now. I have had people, other notable pastors refer to my experiences by comparing them to a cult. Out of respect, I have never called it that. I do not believe that at any time the intent was to hurt people. I believe the intentions were pure and birthed from a true desire to serve God, make people aware of Him, and ultimately keep people from hell. However, without the proper theological context for scripture, we are led by incorrect and damaging interpretations of what scripture is truly saying. When such an approach is taken, it tends to remove the power and focus of what God has given scripture for. The freedom the word is meant to provide, then becomes a chain. I now have a much better understanding and much more compassion regarding how certain things transpired. Over time, the church as a whole has evolved. There is still much work to be done as a body, but having scriptural context provided thorough study and the leading of the Holy Spirit, has helped bring about change. Many things I will speak of, are no longer commonalities among Christian churches. My desire is mainly to provide some perspective on how my own insecurities were established, in the hopes of helping you dig to the bottom of why yours exist.

You got your seat belt on? Okay, let's go for a ride.

My mother and father were excellent parents. They were by no means perfect, but they truly loved their children and were sincere in their efforts to raise us to reverence God, and lead successful lives. Both my dad and mom come from broken, nonreligious homes. They came to Christ in their very early twenties, after getting married at nineteen. My father credits much of his change to being around other honorable men. Much of his influence for being a good husband and father, came from what he witnessed in the church. His own father was absent, and abusive when he was present; he was by no means the greatest example.

Church was a major part of my upbringing. My family went to church ALL THE TIME! Our Sunday mornings, Sunday nights, Tuesday nights, Wednesday nights, and Friday nights, were all spent in church. Not to mention choir rehearsal days, seven-day-long revivals and conventions, and the occasional "shut-ins" where we spent 24 hours in church, praying. Our extra-curricular activities involved what took place at church; anything that conflicted with church would not get our participation.

"Gosh! You're always at church!" My friends would say, and they were right. Church was the number one priority for my family; it was what mattered most. The idea was that the more we went, the closer we were to having a significant relationship with God and becoming who we were meant to be. Growth as Christians was just as dependent on church attendance, as it was any of the other variables taught in regard to God and salvation.

Our constant church attendance was not a major issue then, nor is it now. Church was actually enjoyable because of the friendships that were created there. At the time, most Pentecostal churches had demanding schedules like the one mentioned above; it was normal for many of us to be in church all the time. However, what made church difficult for me and took me years to detox from, was the rule-based, strict, legalistic, theological teaching, that was ingrained in me. Unlike my parents, I was born and being raised in the church. I didn't have the choice or opportunity to learn anything different from what I was taught. I was more familiar with everything God hated and what I could not do, than with what God loved and what I could do. The love of God was talked about maybe 10% of the time, but sin and God's punishment for it, was the main focus.

We had to walk a very fine line in observance of our faith. Women could not wear pants, earrings, excessive jewelry, tank tops or arm bearing shirts, makeup, or nail polish, nor could we cut our hair. The skirts we wore, regardless of length, had to be worn with hosiery. There was to be no bare or exposed skin. Modesty was championed; the more modest you were, the holier you were perceived to be. I wanted so badly to be a cheerleader in middle school, but because of the length of the skirts, I was not able to. Men couldn't have beards, and couldn't wear shorts, tank tops, or necklaces. They'd be outside at church functions, in 90-degree weather playing basketball, fully clothed and soaking wet from the excess sweat. They were also forbidden from having haircuts that included deep parts or design patterns. When we went on church trips, pool time was divided between men and women, and women had to swim with long t-shirts overlaying our swimsuits.

The rules did not just stop with attire and appearance, they reached deep into every area of our lives. Activities such as the going to the movie theater, skating rinks (with the exception of Gospel skate night), and bowling alleys, were frowned upon because of the potential exposure to things that were "worldly," like secular music, smoking, and drinking. Playing card games or "gambling cards," was forbidden. To this day, I don't know how to play card games, with the exception of Uno. I'll smoke you in a game of Uno, but it stops there. The rules extended deep into the structure of the family. There was quite a bit of separation between family and friends who didn't believe the way we did. "…come out from among them, and be ye separate…" *(King James Version, 2 Cor. 6.17)*. This was the scripture taught. Nobody ever explained how we were supposed to show people Jesus, if we couldn't be around them (scratches head).

There were also many unspoken rules. We were greatly discouraged from visiting other churches that were not affiliated with our church, or from building relationships with believers outside of our church. In order to visit another church for ANY reason, permission had to be requested. Permission was often denied based on differing beliefs between the churches. It didn't matter that they served the same Jesus, believed in the same Bible, spoke in tongues, and loved God, there was always a reason we couldn't go. Some things were never blatantly said, but they were clearly taught against, which served as a means to discourage people from leaving the church. The fear was that by allowing members to visit other churches, they would be exposed to different ways of serving God, thus seeing different possibilities that would cause them to leave. When people leave church, so does their money, and though rarely admitted, THIS is, in many cases, the real issue. Members who'd eventually left, some for legitimate reasons and not out of offense, were ostracized, criticized, blacklisted, called "off," another term used for being out of your mind, and said to have missed the mark. Other people who felt the call to evangelize or start churches of their own, received the same treatment. Many tried remaining attached to the fellowship of the church, but were given the "cold shoulder" if they didn't receive permission to go forward in their endeavors, which was only given to a very small number of people. The fear was that members would leave to join churches that previous members started. People with opportunities for out-of-state employment that would provide better security for their family, or that would change their work hours, causing them to attend church less frequently, were encouraged not to take them. It didn't matter that they still served God. If they eventually returned, they were still scrutinized and untrusted—they were treated like traitors.

There were also rules regarding dating and marriage. Young people were encouraged not to wait a long time to get married, especially once they started dating someone. The temptation to "fall into sin" or to fornicate, was far too great. Self-control and discipline were highly suggested, but it was better to marry than to burn. It became the norm for many couples to get married fairly young, that way they could have all of the sex they wanted. The only problem was, once married, they were still being given rules for the marital bed. Certain activities, especially oral sex, was taught against, frowned upon, and even labeled as whoredom and sin, much to the disappointment of the male population. The guys who had been in church their entire lives were eager to experience God's wonder called Eve, so imagine the men who had not grown up in church, who were new converts. They were informed that pre-marital sex was a sin. They had to wrap their minds around the idea of going cold-turkey. Then,

81

they wanted a wife, because, boy oh boy, cold-turkey was really cold. All of those cold showers were for the birds. They wanted to return back to the "land of joy" that beckoned to their man parts, so they got wives. Once married, they were told it was okay to have sex, but there were guidelines for where their mouths could touch. Certain holes were off limits, and you dare not bypass a woman's time of the month and have sex anyway. This was very difficult for some married couples. The rules resulted in a lot of premature marriages. People got married who had no business doing so.

The interference of the church in the marital bed became a major issue. Friction and frustration were followed by contention and strife, and eventually, some marriages ended in divorce. There were many people who stayed together, including my parents, who are still happily married to this day. But for those who could not agree, the tension of finances, sexual frustration, wayward children, the constant battle with sin, and the process of being married and becoming one, were all too much. I know some may be wondering what I, as a pastor, think about this topic, and what scripture says about it. In short, the Bible says the marriage bed is undefiled *(Heb. 13.4)*. In essence, what happens there is between husband and wife, just as long as they are in agreement with one another. Many of the couples who remained married through these things, were in agreement concerning whether or not they would follow the teachings. If you're married, it doesn't matter what I think, all that matters is what you and your spouse agree on. There are still certain things that are clearly outlined in the Bible, and that the Holy Spirit will caution you on concerning your marriage; however, the entrance of other parties and external influences, can result in division that cannot be controlled because of its nature and the fruit it produces. The reality is, if you and your spouse decide that you want to dress up like fairies and ponies, roll around in your bed, pour ketchup and ranch on one another, or streak throughout your house like members of a nudist colony, GO FOR IT! I don't need to know. I don't want to know. Some of you are just weird, but it's okay for you to be weird with your spouse.

The rules were tough, but even they were not the real issue. It was that everything was a requirement, directly tied to sin, "living holy," and God's approval of us. My sin consciousness was at 100%. I was consumed with trying to reach a standard that, in reality, I could never reach. God had to reach it for me by sending His son to die for my sins. I was constantly exhausted mentally and spiritually, dealing with negative thoughts about myself. Not only did it create an atmosphere of extreme self-criticism, but also criticism of others. Not following the list of rules was a sin because it was a direct violation of scripture and church leadership. You might be thinking: *What scripture?* Let me tell you something about people: we can find ANYTHING to support what we believe. This is especially true of Christians. As my husband often says, "Many Christians search the scriptures to find support for what they already believe, not for what they should believe." For the sake of time, I won't run down the many scriptures used, because this is not about a theological debate; however, one specific memory still stings to this day.

From the age of puberty, girls were taught to transition into skirts only. My sister and I, being two years apart, had entered the skirt-only phase around ages 11 and 13. Our pants were thrown out, and the few we were allowed to keep, were only to be worn in the house. I remember a family member giving us a bag of hand-me-downs. There were many things in the bag, including a few pair of pants. My sister and I were elated. My mother, who had not been raised in church, didn't think it was a big deal for us to keep them, so, gradually, my sister and I began wearing them in the house, then outside to play, then on walks to the store, and eventually to school. I'd only been given two pairs from the bag, but I was grateful. I wore the living daylights out of them. I was happy to finally be able to blend in with classmates again. I was really good at sports, but sliding into home plate with a *Little House On the Prairie* skirt on, put me at an immediate disadvantage. I'd be on the basketball court in gym class with a Detroit Pistons jersey and an ankle-length, button-up denim skirt, and those double-strapped, Velcro gym shoes of mine, looking like a confused child. I was constantly teased or questioned by classmates who would ask, "Why do you guys only wear skirts?!" I'd lie and say, "Because I like them!" When you're 40, this seems like nothing, who cares anyway? It's different though, when you're 11 and 13—it's everything! At those ages, you absolutely care what your classmates think. To not have to be weird, and defend my skirt-wearing self, was liberating. By wearing pants more, we were eventually spotted in them by someone from church. "The Parker Girls" had been spotted out-and-about, in pants. This type of information was gold. A tattle-tale opportunity of this magnitude equated to about 10 brownie points. It made me think about when my mom had spotted a deacon from the church, in the lottery line at Farmer Jack. This was another forbidden sin. Gosh, tattling about this could have easily earned my mom a nice 50 brownie points. Gambling was absolutely non-negotiable. Nobody could ever tell me why spending 40 dollars trying to win a bear at the theme park, was any different from gambling or playing the lottery. It was strictly forbidden, yet, here was one of the church deacons posted in line, waiting on his shot to win the Mega Millions. He was a fairly light-skinned man and hard to miss. When he realized my mother had spotted him, he turned every shade of red. My mother was also embarrassed having seen him there, and probably worried about having to report this grievance to the powers that be. They'd seen each other, though, and it was too late to act like they hadn't. Since the cat was now out of the bag, with all of her natural ability, my mom walked over to the deacon and said "Hello." He told her he was there to get lottery tickets for his mother. I was a little kid who didn't know much of anything at the time, but even I could look at him and tell that, if he were attached to a lie detector, sirens and whistles would be going off. Clearly he was lying through his chattering, stuttering teeth. But, the honest truth is, sin or not, had he won, there wasn't a church in the world that wouldn't have gladly accepted ten percent of his winnings. My mother never told anyone except my dad. She was gracious by nature; however, the same couldn't be said of everyone else, so when my sister and I were spotted in our pants, leadership was informed. In turn, my mom and dad received a call.

I will NEVER, I mean NE- to the -E-VER, forget the conversation that ensued and how it made me feel. It was so bad, that the feeling of helplessness is attempting to surface as I write. My mom and dad came into our bedroom and asked us to sit down. I sat on my yellow, green, white, and orange comforter, that my mother had crocheted, as my sister sat down next to me, each of us with concern in our eyes. The looks on my parents' faces were sheepish and somewhat solemn.

"Girls, we're going to have to take the pants back," my dad said.

"Noooooo!!!! Whhhyyyyyy?!?!" My sister, the most dramatic soul to walk the earth, let out a sound someone would howl if their leg was suddenly amputated. She was absolutely horrified. Any composure I had, was soon lost when I looked at my sister, then back

84

at my parents, and realized they were serious, and even worse, there would be no convincing them otherwise.

"Why?!" I asked. They explained the teaching of the church concerning pants, and referenced the scripture that says "a man is not to wear that which pertains to a woman, nor a woman to wear that which pertains to a man" *(Deut. 22.5)*. We were usually really respectful kids who did not talk back, lest we lose our lives, but we'd tasted a little bit of freedom, and it was quickly slipping away. We were willing to risk it all for the cause. My sister and I responded quickly: "Well, they make women pants! These are girl pants," we said, pointing at each other's pants, "no man would wear these! It's not fair!" My dad looked cornered and knew we were right.

"The bible says to obey those that have rule over you. It is the teaching of our church, and we're ministers in this church. We have to obey our leaders," my mom and dad said, after going back and for with my sister and me. With that, our sweet little pants were taken, never to be seen again. My sister and I cried for hours. We sobbed with heaving chests, gasping for air. There was unison in our weeping and gnashing of teeth. We declined dinner that night; we'd completely lost our appetites. We both snuggled under our covers and cried ourselves to sleep. Having shared a room our entire lives, my sister and I were now in the beginning teenage stages, where we fought and argued constantly; however, this situation was different. We found commonality in the situation, that ultimately united us for the time being. We weren't only hurt, but ANGRY. My mother came into the room later to hug me. I could see guilt in her eyes. I knew she meant well. My sister and I stopped speaking to our parents for a week, until my mother informed us that the grace period to have an attitude with her was up, and that she'd politely "knock the living daylights" out of us if we continued in that manner. We decided that the offense wasn't worth being knocked sideways. I'm reminded of how good it felt to be consoled by my mom and to feel her sympathy, but it was too late; I had too many questions now, and no one's answer seemed right.

Something happened to my sister and me that day. It had nothing to do with the pants. It was the fact that we now knew that everything we were following, was because someone was telling us to. I'd looked into my parents' eyes and saw that they, too, disagreed, but as ministers of the church, had to abide by the rules. I made up my mind, in that moment, that something wasn't right. For the first time, something wasn't adding up. I'd gone behind the scenes, and what I'd witnessed birthed distrust and resentment in my heart. The sorrow of having finally fit in with everyone, only to go back to being the weird kid and having to explain myself, was too much. I didn't know what was right or wrong anymore. I thought about every birthday party or family function we'd abruptly left, when secular music started playing. I thought about all the seemingly harmless movies and television shows we couldn't watch, because of kissing or possible witchcraft relations. I remembered other Christians who didn't believe like we did and opted out of following our strict set of rules. We were strongly discouraged from befriending them or attending their churches. I thought about everything, and the more we were told no and reminded of sin, the more my curiosity and desire peaked.

As my curiosity peaked, I employed other methods to do what I desired to. My sister and I did a lot of sneaking around. We'd sneak pants and clip-on earrings into our backpacks, and change when we got to school. My aunt had given me a tube of cherry red lip gloss, that could pass as lipstick. I slapped it on my lips, along with lip liner and cheap pink blush for my cheeks. We did whatever we could to pass for normal. I knew it was direct disobedience to my parents' instructions, and according to the teaching of my church, it was a sin to disobey your mom and dad. *Spray me down with gasoline, and load me into a canon,* I thought; I was on my way to hell. This is how I felt every morning I woke up, until I laid my head down at night. I was hell bound. On several occasions people stood before the entire church to repent of their sins after they'd been found out or confessed. A few girls who had gotten pregnant out of wedlock, someone caught wearing earrings, and a man who'd been caught wearing a chain, were all put before the congregation, then had to sit out for a period of time, without serving. I remember the shame, sorrow, and indignation I felt for them, as they apologized to a church full of people who had their own issues, but had simply not been caught or reported yet. I dreaded such an experience, but felt it was inevitable because of my sinfulness.

Imagine carrying this mentality from age 9 all the way to age 33. Twenty-four years of my life were spent in constant condemnation and fear. I repented every day, all day long, for my sins. I begged God not to let me die in my sins because I didn't want to spend an eternity in hell. It produced constant insecurity, fear, and terror. I remember losing sight of my mother in the shopping center one day: she'd left me and went over to another store, unbeknownst to me. For the five minutes I couldn't find her, I thought the rapture had taken place. She was nowhere in sight and neither were any babies, nuns, priests, or anyone with long skirts and bare faces. Everywhere I looked, I saw hellions, so I thought I'd been left behind. I absolutely lost it. I was running up and down aisles, from store to store, hollering for my momma, until finally, I started crying. By the time my mother found me, I was preparing to dig a tunnel to hide during the tribulation period.

My formative years were spent in shame. I didn't know what to do with all my feelings and emotions, that I now know to be, quite frankly, normal to children and human beings in general. Being a singer, I would hear secular music and would be unable to get it out of my head. Melodies and rhythms quickly attached to my ear, and I loved what I was hearing. My sister and I had been punished on a few occasions for sneaking secular tapes into the house. It made me feel dirty; I thought there was something wrong with me. There had to be something wrong with me because what I was doing was a sin, but I liked it. During puberty, sexual feelings towards boys arose, which also made me feel dirty and ashamed. In an effort to fit in at school, I'd sometimes use profanity. I had to work harder than normal to be accepted, and it often required behavior contrary to what I saw at home—behavior that was not a true representation of my natural personality. Attributes of my natural personality, like humor and whit, were over-emphasized. I became the class clown in order to satisfy feelings of inadequacy. It also didn't help that when my behavior switched, some of my church peers I'd known my whole life, were told by their mothers that they couldn't play with me anymore. I was uninvited from a few slumber parties and labeled for a season. Now I'm a grown woman and can still remember how rejected I felt. I can't recall a time where I didn't feel ashamed and dirty.

This carried on for years. I didn't feel like I measured up. I felt like a bad Christian. I felt weak. I felt unaccepted. I felt insecure, and as a man or a woman thinks in their heart, so are they. I did everything I could to avoid these feelings, except come to a God who was the answer to it all, and receive His love for me. I went to God, often; still, deep down inside, I always felt I was a second away from losing His approval. I could never seem to get a sin-free day under my belt. There was always a point in my day that I'd mess up some in way. I lived under perpetual condemnation and shame.

I was not the only one. I'd witnessed these same feelings affect other people, even my siblings. I remember one day, in my early twenties, praying for my sister. She was at a bad point in her life. She'd just had her daughter, was in between jobs, and my niece's father was a considerable issue. I wanted so desperately for her to come to God and receive peace and healing, but every conversation with her resulted in defensiveness. She had a lot of feelings about God and church, and quite frankly, spoke of wanting nothing to do with it all. She was very vocal about wanting to live her life the way she wanted to. As I drove down the road one day, I prayed for her earnestly. The Holy Spirit spoke to my heart very loudly and said, "She's come to believe a lie." I nearly stopped short and picked up my phone to dial her number. I didn't tell her what God had spoken to me, I simply asked, "What are you doing with your life right now, that is so important and worth more than living for God?" She was very quiet, almost too quiet, until I broke the silence.

"Hello! You still there?" I asked.

She cut through, stuttering, with tension and defensiveness in her voice.

"Shaunee, I'm just not like some of these people. I feel like living as a Christian is just easy to do and meant for some people. They are never tempted, and don't have any struggles like me. I just can't do it. I'm not one of those people who can live for God. I am who I am, and I just can't do it."

There it was, the lie. It was a lie we both had come to believe. I was living for God, doing everything I could to walk with Him, and I still believed just like she did. Ultimately, I thought something was wrong with me. I believed then, that I was not, nor would I ever be good enough for God.

What are your immediate thoughts about who God is? What are your immediate thoughts about who He thinks you are? What are your main beliefs concerning religion and how it affects your past, present, and future?

HOME LIFE

"The encouragement of a parent empowers a child, but the discouragement of a parent cripples a child, which leads to insecurities."
- *Bishop Jamie Englehart*

Now that I'm older and have children of my own, I'm better able to evaluate what things must have been like for my parents, raising us. Both of them, having come from broken homes, were somewhat "winging it," trying to raise us completely different and follow God in a way that was pleasing. I see now that many of their own insecurities were at work as they came to God. It was widely taught that dedicating your life and your family's life to God, resulted in blessings. This was taught more than stewardship and other practical things anyone could benefit from, whether they served God or not. God did His part to love and protect our family, but He never overrode an inability to steward life.

There were many times I'd sit and listen to my parents talk about finances and how we were struggling. During his entry-level fireman days, the City of Detroit did layoffs, and my dad was included in the selection. It was a very difficult period. Eventually, he was called back to work, and we were on our feet again. I remember a lot of stress and fear weighing on my father for all the years I lived at home. I don't remember him ever being completely at peace. Money was always an issue, and during our teenage years, we were an issue, too. More than anything else, my dad simply did not want to fail at being a good husband and father—everything his dad wasn't. I don't think he was ever fully confident in his ability to be who he desired to be. His anxiety often reflected his internal fears. He felt that if he couldn't do it, it wouldn't happen. His faith and hope in God were tied to his faithfulness to Him; he was concerned with what his good works could produce. I don't know that he ever truly believed he was secure in God.

I remember being eight years old and waking up in the middle of the night. I walked into the living room to find my dad on his knees, facing the couch. He was weeping, bawling. He was praying and asking God for help—practically begging for help. I distinctly remember him saying, "God, I just want to be able to do for my kids." I stopped in my tracks. My dad was the love of my life, my hero. I'd always perceived him to be big, strong, and athletic, a "Macho Man" of sorts. There was nothing I didn't think my dad could do, and for the first time, I was seeing him cry. It scared me and I felt an overwhelming sense of compassion for him.

"Daddy. Why you crying?" I asked. He turned around stunned, and when he saw me, standing there, barefoot, with two pig tails, in my Cinderella nightgown, he cried even louder and harder. He grabbed me and held me, crying into my gown. I started crying because I didn't know what was wrong with my daddy.

"I'm okay, Shaunee. Don't cry. I'm just a little sad that I couldn't get you guys those bikes today," he finally said. We'd gone to K-Mart earlier that day. All of us kids were getting to the age where we wanted bikes. There was a wide variety of colors, makes, and models, all with streamers and bells. We rode a couple up and down the aisle, begging to get them. My dad put the bikes back on the rack.

"Daddy can't right now. I don't have the money. Maybe later, okay?" He said. We were disappointed, no doubt, but we were kids and had quickly gotten over it. My dad had not. I didn't know it, but it's obvious that he'd driven home with the weight of disappointed in his heart. To him, not having the money for something as simple as bikes for his children, equated to failure. It didn't matter that we thought the world of him. He had his own standards of acceptance, and he'd fallen short of them. This experience still feels like yesterday to me, 30 years later. It imprinted a fear of failure and security on me, almost instantaneously. I am the one, out of four kids, who is the best at managing money. To this day, people ask for my advice concerning budgeting and money management. I'm constantly applauded because of my ability to save and flip a buck. However, the root of this quality started with insecurity, a fear of poverty, and a desire to never experience the feeling that caused a grown man to fall to his knees, crying.

My mom had her insecurities as well. She was overly conscious about how she and our family was perceived. I think deep inside, she nursed an inferiority complex about our economic status. She'd sat back and watched many people blessed with new homes and cars; still, we were struggling. She was also exceptionally private. We were given instruction to never go out of our house and tell any of our parents' business or what went on in our home. Now that I've matured, I've realized that maintaining privacy is important and beneficial, but it was more so my mom's effort to guard our public persona. She never tried passing us off as well-to-do or grandiose, but she never wanted pity or for us to be overlooked. Ultimately, I believe she wanted to be respected, and after being raised in a family where gain equated to respect, that's the way she wanted us to live. She, like my dad, believed our serving God, would eventually lead to a blessing of great magnitude. She often pressed my dad to make financial decisions that weren't the soundest. As a woman of faith by nature, she believed works were required to receive, and she was right. However, with insecurity at the foundation, steps are often taken following its leading, and not the leading of the Holy Spirit. It's a hit or miss when we're directed by anything other than the Holy Spirit, and we had a lot more misses than hits.

I watched my parents make many mistakes with my older sister and brother, as my siblings were openly non-conformists. I also watched them do many things right. I honestly could not have asked for better parents. I have a great deal of affection and love for how they raised us and made continual sacrifices for our benefit. I don't think my parents saw then, or even now, how such a religious structure affected us. Sure, there were some very good things that came out of it; if nothing else, I learned the importance of being sincere with God. It was all or nothing then, and is all or nothing now, but with that type of teaching, most people's commitment was the result of fire insurance; they didn't want to go to hell.

The teachings at church followed us at home. There was a work-then-reward structure, even there. My mom and dad were loving and there was no doubt we were in their hearts constantly, but words of affirmation and encouragement were typically only given in response to good works. Of course they recognized our efforts, but to fail at things that were considered important, meant a verbal lashing would follow. This didn't produce much fruit, but only added to feelings of failure and condemnation. Poor grades were not tolerated, as they should not be, but, in our family, you weren't getting any back rubs or pep talks if you got them; more than likely you'd be shamed. I remember us often being verbally compared to one another. It seemed harmless, but when you're the one on the bottom being told to climb up to your sibling's level, it feels crappy. Sure, there was fun, laughter, and lots of family moments, but they were all spent walking on pins and needles, because you were always one second away from failure again.

The love of God was only spoken of in response to good deeds or if you lived according to His word. Messages from church about sinners, hell, and all the rebuke associated with it, were reiterated at home. I have no memories of being introduced to the love of God—the presence of God, yes, but not His love. I was always led to believe that His presence was there because I'd done something right, never because He simply loved ME. The good things spoken about God were wonderful, but not enough to balance or remove the fear that came as a result of the other teachings. The internal insecurity my parents felt, was projected on us. I grew up under it, and the one insecurity I had concerning God, turned into insecurity about everything, especially myself. I didn't think much of myself, and my criticism of others, reflected how I felt about myself. It stayed with me for years, and in transitional periods of my life, may surface if left unchecked. I am still learning much about God and His love for me. You never stop learning. There is no point where it goes away because you've "arrived." It's a lifelong process.

With all the good that was done at home, it still didn't eliminate the insecurities that had begun shaping me. All the hugs and kisses did nothing to quench my people-pleasing tendencies, or my craving for acceptance. I craved recognition. I craved love that was not circumstantial. The sad thing is, I had always had it, but never knew it, and when you have something but don't know it, it's the same as not having it. You'll do anything to get it.

It's likely you've read my story and can relate. You may be the person who thinks I need to shut up, because my little story pales in comparison to yours. It does not matter the extent of what has caused our insecurities. The only thing that matters is that the insecurities are present, and will continue to cause damage. Maybe you were sexually abused, raped, violated, physically abused, bullied, verbally abused, ignored, rejected, or hated. Maybe it was a failed marriage or relationship that sealed your pain. Maybe it was going through a divorce or watching it tear your parents and family apart. Perhaps the loss of a child or loved one has caused you to deny the existence of God, or simply His love for you. No matter what it is, it is imperative that you pinpoint its origin. It's also critical that you get to the root of the lie supporting it. If you can kill the lie, you can kill your insecurity, and once it's dead, it has no more power to cripple you. Pull from within, go to the surface, and look it in its face. See it for everything it is. It doesn't own you. It won't rule you any longer. Exposure is a critical step. Change is near.

Journal Moment

Which memories have surfaced? Write down the memories you believe are a part of your insecurities. Elaborate on any feelings and thoughts, being careful to add all details that emerge, especially those you have not thought about before now.

Hi Insecurity. BYE Insecurity.

7

THE DAMAGES

"Every bad decision that I ever made can be traced back to the presence of insecurity." - Shaunee Brannan

Like most internal struggles, deficiencies, or illnesses in our lives, it is not only the symptoms that cause us discomfort, and alert us to their presence, but it is often what they take from us, and the damage we suffer, that leads us to confront them. I said at the beginning of the book that insecurity is not something you outgrow; it is something you out-know. Your struggle with it can begin in early childhood and follow you all the way to the grave. It's ability to morph and go undercover, is incredible. People who live without accountability, moral standards, or relationships that provide constructive criticism, can go on forever, without facing what lives inside of them. If in denial, the only thing able to pull them out, are rock-bottom experiences. With every fall, failure, or indiscretion, and the consequences that follow, they start to trace back to where the issue first began. After peeling back layers and searching their hearts and intentions, they find that the driving force is an insecurity, screaming to be satisfied.

When we feed our insecurities with coping mechanisms, it is like running from a snake in a house, into a garage with a running car, filled with carbon monoxide. Your perception of danger in one place, leads you to seek refuge in another place, but without knowing it, you often end up in greater danger than the place you ran from. Insecurity slowly peels away at reality, numbing your senses and stealing your joy and ability to think rationally. Desperate to get a handle on stability, you search for a place that resembles you. The problem is, you don't even know who you are yet, and when you don't know who you are, everything becomes an option. Your search to find identify, leads you down paths that feels like home, only for a short time. But, once regret begins to haunt your house, you realize it wasn't your house in the first place.

In the previous chapter, I mentioned it would probably be one of the most transparent and difficult chapters to write; that was before I started writing this one. I did everything I could to get out of writing this.

"Shaunee, you cannot tell that!" I said to myself. "You can get your point across without telling your personal business!" I really could have, but to go around such critical details for the sake of escaping criticism, is a coping mechanism for insecurity, and now that I have the knowledge, I will never feed what was killing me. If you starve it, it will die. After being awakened several nights at 3:30a.m., I knew God was not going to let me rest, until I at least submitted in my heart to sacrificing my supposed dignity and public image, to help free someone. Your victory and healing are worth me giving up every ounce of my pride.

Being able to share my failures is a personal victory. It is something I would have never been able to do 10 years ago. My image, and the way people perceived me still mattered to me in an unhealthy way. I'd been shaped by my insecurities regarding acceptance, and more than anything, the desire to escape shame, that had been placed on me by so many factors. Never feeling good enough, I worked hard to be good enough, but in all the wrong ways. As my insecurities further populated, they gave birth to experiences that cemented their presence. These experiences were like fertilizer on grass, and gasoline on fire. My insecurities grew rapidly, as did my ability to mask them by utilizing coping mechanisms; however, rock bottom was eminent, and God used it to create an opening for Him to rescue me.

There's so much to tell, with so little time. Let's start here......

ALL BECAUSE SHE DIDN'T KNOW SHE WAS PRETTY

"When you don't know who you are, everything is an option."
- Shaunee Brannan

I tried to think back to the first time—the earliest memory I had of it. I remembered being eight years old and receiving a yellow, black, and white plaid dress, complete with white ruffle socks, white patent leather shoes, a pair of white gloves, and a white straw hat, with the matching ribbon, for Easter. My godmother, who didn't have any children, had bought it for me. My mom had pressed my hair straight. I was glowing, as I walked toward the long mirror in the hallway of our

96

house to look at myself. This was the first time I remember being told I was pretty, and I associated every single compliment that I'd gotten that day, with the clothes I had on. Without them, I was average. Being called pretty felt amazing. It felt like recognition. It felt like worth. It felt foreign to me, and I never wanted the feeling to go away.

I don't have many memories of being called pretty in my early years; "cute," "sexy," "fine," yes, I'd heard all of these, but not pretty, and certainly not beautiful. I thought back, and could not remember my mom and dad saying it. My elementary years were awkward. I was cute, but in an average way. I didn't feel special or doted upon. I remember a project in second grade that required us to bring in pictures of ourselves as babies. I'd heard my parents and family members talk about my sister and me as babies, while looking at family photo albums. They always mentioned how cute my sister had been, how beautiful of a baby she was, but never mentioned me in the same way. That's why, when it was time to take a photo, I switched out the picture my mother had given me, for one of my sister's. After seeing the picture, everyone in class talked about how cute of a baby I was, but said, "... it looks nothing like you!" To which I'd reply, defensively, "Well, it is me!" At eight years old, my mind had concluded I wasn't pretty.

To make matters worse, in fourth grade, my mother complained about how difficult it was to manage my hair, which was much thicker and coarse than my sister's. As a result, she took me to the hair dresser and got me a Leisure Curl, also known as a "Jerri Curl" that consisted of slightly thicker curls. It shrunk my hair up and with big glasses on my face, I looked like a 65-year-old black man from the south, who liked Jazz, Bourbon, and cigars. When I showed up at school with my hair like that, my archrival, BJ, hollered out: "Look everybody! It's B.B. King," the famous Blues guitarist. That hairstyle was a bad idea. Then, as puberty hit, I started getting my dad's mustache. I would sneak and shave the corners of it every three weeks. I was super conscious of every flaw. I was good at sports and an honor roll student. I received a lot of praise and recognition from classmates for that, but especially from my dad. It was my supplement at the time.

Then there came the age where I started liking boys. Even with my insecurities, I was still a leader by nature. Being popular and witty got me a few playground dates, but the one boy I liked, really liked, told me to my face that he didn't think I was cute. It wouldn't have mattered if I didn't already think that myself, but I did. It put such a complex in me that increased my fear of rejection. At age 11, I had my back turned at the Detroit Auto Show and a grown man in his twenties, walked past me.

"DANG! That little girl got a big butt! Do you see her butt?" He hollered out to his friends. This was the first time references to my body were made. I developed very early and was clueless about what my body looked like and what it meant to men, prior to this encounter. As time went on, it became more and more common for men to reference my body. I was built much like my mother and grandmother—a real brickhouse. I had a small waist, big hips, and round butt, all at 11 years old. All of a sudden, I became much more interesting to boys. My sassy personality and take-charge attitude, were also attractive; still, I didn't like being objectified or sexualized. I wasn't really a "fast" girl; I was quite innocent and sheltered, having been watched very closely by my parents, to prevent me from being harmed. Comments about my body made me feel disgusting, but I liked the attention. I liked being put above the rest, so I adopted a "look, but don't touch" mentality, because I didn't want to lose the feeling attention gave to me.

By the time I was in high school, I'd learned how to alter my look to compensate for what I felt like I lacked. I'd ride my bike to the beauty supply store to buy a pack of $4.99 weave, and after getting a perm, I'd do my own hair. I remember the first time I sneaked into my mother's drawer and found her jet black, Cleopatra wig. When she'd leave us home alone to go get groceries, I'd get some Vaseline and smack it on my lips, then put the wig on and parade in front of the mirror, singing and making gestures. I thought I was smoking hot. I made up my mind that this was how I wanted to look. When I started making my own money, I bought more weave. My mother wasn't really monitoring my hair or what I did to it, as long as she didn't have to do it, and I didn't ask to cut it (church rules). She never assessed the damage I was doing to it. By age 24, after all the harsh, glue and chemical-filled hairstyles I'd worn, most of my hair was damaged beyond repair. The natural hair movement was not in place during those years. My natural hair would have been considered "nappy" and out of trend. In my insecurity, I made fun of different classmates with "natural" hair. My weaves provided me a sense of control over my appearance and how I was perceived. Today, "naturals" are more accepted, partly because of worldwide insecurity, and the convenience they provide for people, like who I used to be, to cover their own damage. This is a difficult topic to discuss. I mourned the damage of my hair for years.

I just want to remind you, supplementing our insecurities is like a fertilizer: It feeds them so they can grow and populate. One small insecurity about my hair, turned into a larger one. As I continued adding to my insecurities, I found multiple ways to supplement. At some point in my life, I've used just about every coping mechanism mentioned in Chapter 5. I was jealous, envious, competitive, judgmental, and critical of others. In moments where I felt inadequate, I did whatever necessary to feel better about myself.

By the time I'd gotten to high school, I'd mastered doing things I needed to do to feel better about myself. Every chance I got, I would spend my babysitting money on clothes. The way I dressed had become a large part of my self-acceptance. The way people looked at me when I put these clothes on, made me feel euphoric. Witnessing envy from other women as they stared me up and down, was magical. I knew the look. I'd given it to so many because of my jealousy-fueled heart. I loved it.

I'd learned how to steal what I couldn't buy. I started shoplifting at five years old. The first time, I stole a vial of ChapStick from the grocery store, after my dad told me several times that I could not get it. At five, I was quite ignorant, so each time my dad turned his back, I'd slather the ChapStick on. By the time we got to check-out, I looked like a shining Thanksgiving Day turkey. My dad paid for the ChapStick, threw it in the trashcan, in my face, then whipped my butt in the car. Did I do it again? YEP! I was 12 years old, and at the mall with friend who'd convinced me to steal three pairs of Mickey Mouse socks, that were very popular at the time, from Mervyn's. We thought we were in the clear, until security walked up to us and politely took us in the back office to wait for my father, who was called in lieu of the police. When he walked in, the look on his face let me know I was in for a whirlwind. For those that don't believe in spankings, skip to the next paragraph. I got my behind whipped, and although it didn't solve my problem, it was a standard in our house. We got spankings, but the punishment wasn't enough to keep me from doing it again, and again, and again. To take that supplement from me, would have put me back at ground zero. Without all my supplements, I felt average. I'd come too far and was being praised too much; there was no way could I lose the momentum.

When people are insecure, they pull from wherever they can to find validation. The older I got the better I became at covering my insecurities; I pulled from everywhere. I was praised for how I looked and how I sang. My unique factor and God-given purpose, could be seen, even beyond my faults. People were drawn to it, even when they didn't know that's what they saw in me. I didn't know that's what it was. I know now, but then, I attributed it to all of the hard work I was putting in "to become." "Becoming" is so hard when you're using artificial things. I never got there, I only appeared to be there.

At age 18, right after graduating from high school, I gave my heart to God. Right there in my living room, I made the decision to stop running from Him and to give Him everything. Was I ever really running from Him? No. I'd always wanted God. I just didn't think He'd wanted me. I didn't think I could live for Him and give up everything the rules required. All the peer pressure I was exposed to in high school, was too much. I'd conformed to everyone else, who was trying to conform to me for acceptance. I was the leader trying to impress my followers (Saul), and my conformity paid off. I won Prom Queen by a landslide, in addition to several categories in the "Most..." portion of our yearbook. People who are insecure always categorize others by their own insecurities. All those empty accolades meant everything to me at the time. They were my chosen supplements.

At age 19, I began traveling the world singing background for different gospel artists. I went from traveling within a 25-mile radius, to traveling all over America and many other parts of the world. I began getting a lot of recognition and praise from my local church. They were genuinely happy for me. What happened for me, happened for them, as I had been a lifelong member, and many of them had known me as a child. It brought a new level of respect and validity to not only my gift, but who I was. This was my next supplement. "She must be somebody special if..." People would say. Those who'd never spoken to me before, were speaking to me now. I got lots of pats on the back, and more solos in the choir. My life changed drastically; I was living a dream. Initially, I was shell-shocked. I was living for God with everything I had. Prayer, fasting, and church—lots of it, were substantial parts of my life. I was experiencing love and acceptance from God at a level I had never imagined. Still, I attributed all of my blessings, even living a dream, to my good behavior. I was immediately put into an atmosphere of other believers who lived everyday lives, much different than what I'd known, or had lived. Some of them had something substantial with God, while others struggled. I was very conflicted about how they were "Christians," who cursed when angry, had marital problems and were on the verge of divorce, listened to secular music, and were lusty and disconnected from God. Yet, the presence of God was undeniable in rehearsals and performances. Actually, I'd never experienced worship that was as real as when with these people. Every bit of it defied my belief that God didn't dwell with imperfect people. I cried myself to sleep in my bunk on the tour bus several times, asking God for answers. They didn't come then, but they did come later, in my greatest failures.

PRETTY IS MY NAME

I'd fallen in love with this new life and all it was exposing me to. I was meeting new people and starting to get a solid handle on my maturing appearance. At this point, all of my acne had completely disappeared, bearing flawless brown skin, a bright smile with straight teeth that had never required braces, and my body had never looked better. I'd overhear conversations about me all the time when I'd walk by men. I was finally being called "pretty" all the time. I was constantly pursued. Men would call the studio where I worked, after seeing me in videos or at concerts. Some men would go as far as to follow our bus back to the hotel to meet me. Among these men were professional athletes and men of status. Whatever potential I'd had before, I had never seen. Sure, I'd been complimented within my circle, but I was beginning to discover that Shaunee was a big deal. Who knew? You have to understand what this felt like for the little girl that still lived inside me. The little girl from Detroit, with the B.B. King curls and the mustache. I felt like my beauty was very fragile, and that it could have easily been taken away. I worried about losing what made me appealing. I felt that my line between desirable, and undesirable was very thin. Every time I was called "pretty," it was like a stream trickling into a dry spot on the ground. It was hard to accept or believe, but I was hearing it repeatedly. As I started to believe it, my head got as big as the Goodyear Blimp. My supplementing began backfiring.

Of course my body was always a topic of conversation. I didn't have to work out. I ate whatever I wanted and my stomach stayed flat. My hips and butt were the perfect proportions. I was very self-conscious about being lusted after by men. I'd allowed that type of attention to poison my thinking in high school, and I was now in a place with God where I wanted to feel as pure as I was living. I'd done everything I could to keep from feeling the shame associated with sin and being "dirty," that I thought I'd escape by living committed to God. Still, it remained. Subconsciously, it was still there. I covered up as much as possible, trying to remain modest, but because much of my service to God was bred out of ignorance and imperfect theology, I was ill-equipped for reality and the knowledge of the choices I had. I didn't understand gray areas and consequences. I was naïve and ignorant, in the worst ways.

Eventually, I ended up meeting someone during my travels. I was dating someone else at the time, but as my head got bigger, so did my opinion of who I should be with. When you're insecure, you don't waste any opportunity for supplements that could potentially support deficiencies. The new guy I'd met was well-known and reputable. Dating him was an attention grabber. Since he was more appealing, I mercilessly dumped my boyfriend, a genuinely good guy, who loved God and me. In turn, I started dating someone as weak and insecure as I was. He was immature, materialistic, had major identity issues, and was much older than me. He'd already been married and divorced, and had two kids. His level of experience in life, far out-matched mine. I was not equipped to handle the amount of manipulation and deception that followed me entertaining this man.

The subliminal pressure for sex began almost immediately. It caused a lot of discord, arguing, and indecisiveness on my part. I'd break up with him, and allow myself to be wooed back, time after time. The fighting was intense and provoked irrational behavior, such as him chasing my car by foot, down the street for two blocks, screaming and begging me to come back. I would think: *This must be love!* At the time, I was too insecure to see it as emotional instability. I did, however, stand my ground on not having sex. I genuinely loved God, like REALLY loved Him. We had something real and I didn't want to ruin it, but as time went on, the pressure increased. I would get angry and break up with him. He'd repent, play the role, and win me back. This went on for at least a year. I withheld for a year. We'd travel together and sleep in the same bed, which is a dangerous thing to do, but even then, I withheld. In my heart, it wasn't always a struggle. I really didn't want to slip back into that trap. I'd lost my virginity at 15, the same way, under peer pressure, not because I wanted to. I was never a naturally lustful person. I didn't crave sex, had not been promiscuous, and had never masturbated. That was not my struggle, but with time, my walls were being chipped away little by little, until I eventually gave in.

It wasn't romantic or enjoyable, and immediately afterward, I felt ashamed, dirty, and an enormous amount of regret. I laid replaying what had happened in my mind. I was in shock. I couldn't believe it. It had come and gone just like that, and just like most Christians who fall into similar traps, we were unprepared and had no protection, but I was going to fix it. We made a vow that day, to never do it again. We prayed—I mean, I prayed, and asked God to forgive us and to strengthen us. Turns out we'd need it. Four weeks later, I sat in a free clinic in Atlanta, the last one of eight women called into the office, after receiving a free pregnancy test. The lady looked me right in the eye and said, "So I take it you already know you're pregnant, right?"

IF I MAKE MY BED IN HELL

The walk to the car and the ride back to his apartment felt like an eternity. I couldn't cry because I couldn't breathe. He was talking to me, but I couldn't hear a word. I stared straight ahead, passing scenery, cars, people, and seeing none of it. I was having an out-of-body experience. My mind was flooded with a million thoughts, as fear and terror began to overtake me. My mind settled on what everyone at church would say. Just nine months before, I'd watched a terrified 17-year-old girl stand before the church, sobbing and weeping, asking the congregation for forgiveness, because she'd gotten pregnant out of wedlock. Her mother stood beside her, head hung low, both clearly in shame. I'd sat in the congregation, horrified, wanting to hug her, to rescue her, but this was standard for those who had been caught in sin. After receiving the news, I sat in the car thinking, I'm next. I pictured myself right where she stood, repenting, in shame. I didn't think about what my mom and dad would say. I didn't think about how I would raise a baby or get married to this guy. The first and most predominant thought in my mind was: *I cannot go back and face those people.* This thought alone, sent me into a tailspin. Image was everything to me. What people thought about me was paramount. The more I pictured myself having to go ten months with a baby in my stomach, and ten months facing "those people," the more I realized I couldn't. After only a few minutes of riding and thinking, I'd made up my mind. I turned to him and said, "I want an abortion."

That next morning at 5:00a.m., as we drove to the clinic, I was still in shock. He'd tried all night to convince me to change my mind, mostly because he feared losing me. He figured a baby would secure his place in my life, but we'd never know. The fear of my sin being uncovered, was my persuader. At 6:00a.m., when I was four weeks pregnant, on a cold, metal gurney, facing a masked man, I had an abortion.

Back at his place, I lay on the ground, freshly showered in my pajamas and in a fetal position. I was still in shock. It took some time, but I finally broke. The reality of the last year and how I had sunk to this point, shook me. I cried my eyes out. The pain and bleeding were substantial, but it was the internal pain I felt, that hurt the most. The joy of not having to face people was there, but there wasn't enough of it to outweigh my reality. I held myself and cried. At first I couldn't speak, but finally, after hours of lying there, I finally said, "God…please…" I couldn't get the rest out. "God…please…I'm sorry. Please forgive me." I felt incredulous even asking. My heart was in shambles. I felt like I'd given up on something so real with God. I was at my lowest, dirtiest, most shameful and disgraceful point, and out of nowhere, like a flood, came this overwhelming presence. The TV was blaring, but I couldn't hear it. I could literally feel the presence of God, full of peace and love, and it overwhelmed me. I felt loved, cared for, and FORGIVEN. I cried like a baby. This presence defied everything I'd come to believe about God and sin. I'd ruined my life, and taken another. Still, here He was, holding me, being the best example of a father.

CHECK YOUR WOUNDS

Our insecurities, just like all sickness, leave trails and signs of damage in our lives. It supplements, only to further create a deficiency. It fertilizes a seed so fruit can spring up from it, in order for it to eat to survive. It is an ongoing cycle of dysfunction, hurt, and pain. Perhaps you are nothing like me. Maybe your damages are mild and you're thinking: *I wasn't a murderer!* Neither was I, until insecurity told me it was my only option. Insecurity became my leading. It replaced the voice of God and my morals, and stole my choices from me. It became my identity. That's how it operates.

Perhaps your story is the same, if not worse than mine. Maybe your insecurity led to promiscuity. Maybe you found yourself in a pattern of crime or violence to satisfy it. Maybe you turned to food addictions or substance abuse to numb the memories. Maybe you were the person to steal away and become a hermit, to avoid people altogether. No matter how you chose to supplement your deficiency, there is still a trail. When we use artificial means to deal with something natural, it does not accomplish what we hope. Instead, it creates more problems than the original issue. It's just like the infomercials. You have trouble sleeping and see an infomercial for "Nighty-Nite." The infomercial shows people having trouble sleeping, tossing and turning just like you. After taking "Nighty-Nite," people are seen waking up from a long night's rest, refreshed, playing catch with their kids and working efficiently, as if their problem is solved. Then, in a much lower tone, a voice says, "Nighty-Nite will solve your sleeping problems, but may cause temporary blindness, numbness in your hands, legs, arms, neck, face – heck, your whole body will go out on you, be prepared when this happens. It may also cause nightmares, diarrhea, nausea, vomiting, barking like a dog, baldness, sweaty arm pits, trapped gas, and lockjaw." Still, for some of us, the idea of getting sleep, outweighs other potential danger and side effects.

That's exactly what happens when we take our insecurity into our own hands; we solve one symptom, only to populate many more. In the years my husband and I have been pastors to people, I wish I could count the people we've counseled with severe insecurity, that has ruled their lives. As a result of the trauma many of them have suffered (rape, incest, domestic violence, sexual crimes, rejection, abandonment, bullying, etc.), they carried on with life because they felt they had to, but they never received healing. Their security was robbed from them, leaving them insecure and vulnerable. Sexual confusion, promiscuity, pornography, illegal activity, violence, and substance abuse, became the means by which they endured and numbed their pain. I've had to talk many people off the ledge; each one, running from their insecurity or the consequences of supplementing them. The damage we suffer from insecurity, has a way of bringing us all to our knees, even those who are in denial about their conditions. It has a way of breaking you down and showing you that your way was never and will never be the way. It's a good thing. Those damages are the things that will make you ready, willing, and hopeful for the cure.

Journal Moment

Consider your insecurities, both past and present, and the damages they caused. How did you deal with them? How are you dealing with them now? Have you faced them the right way? Are you ready to face them now?

8

THE CURE

"And be not conformed to this world, but be ye transformed by the renewing of your mind, so that you can prove what the will of God is, that which is good, and acceptable and perfect." - Romans 12:2, NASB

The cure, the cure, the cure. I wish a magic pill existed. I wish there was some sort of medical procedure possible where they cut us open, go into our brains and hearts, and extract all of our fears and failures. But, there isn't. A cure isn't that simple and never will be. As a matter of fact, a permanent cure doesn't exist. I think I just heard you let out a cuss word. You may be thinking: *Shaunee, you mean to tell me, you had me buy this little rinky dink book and read through several chapters, only to inform me that a cure doesn't exist?* No, that's not what I said, Shugah. I said a *permanent* cure doesn't exist. There will never come a time in your life where insecurity doesn't try to rear its head in some way. You may never stop confronting it, but, there is a cure for your dysfunction, pain, wounds, and thinking. When those areas receive the necessary healing and attention, insecurity does not carry the same weight; it is not as big of a threat to you as it once was. It becomes more circumstantial than characteristic. It becomes easier to deal with externally, having been conquered internally. We are not looking to cure your insecurity—we are looking to cure you. Remember, it all goes back to how you see God and yourself. If your perception is in alignment to truth, insecurity, and anything else that is foreign to that nature, will be detoxed as you transform. You will only be as whole and healed, as you are connected to God and yourself. This is what the cure consists of:

1. Transparency
2. Letting God in
3. Truth
4. Identity
5. Walking in the Spirit
6. Repeat steps 1-5 over and over again. Daily. Habitually. Reverently.

I'm sure there may be some who are struggling with their faith in God, or even those who are Agnostic or Atheist, who may be reading this. Many of you may have tried the "God thing," and feel you've simply failed at it, over and over again. Others may be angry or offended at God—I was at several points in my life. Giving Him another chance seemed like a pointless thing to do. The temptation to skip over this part or erect walls of defense, is not something I'm going to try convincing you not to do. Instead, I will continue sharing details of my life, in the hopes of showing you much of His reality. You can continue to be the judge.

It took a few more alarming realizations for me to accept the truth of the relationship I was in. After loaning him money, maxing out two credit cards, and a few rumors of him cheating, I finally ended the relationship that had taken me on a journey to death. I had been brought to my lowest. I'd had enough with self-medicating. I was ready and willing. I wanted a cure. Let me be clear, I do not want to give the impression that I'm blaming my insecurity on a toxic relationship; this is a common mistake that we make. We believe that ending something toxic, deals with our insecurities, or that our insecurities result from toxic relationships. Here's the truth: the relationship only fed what was already there. The relationship gave me another outlet to operate in my insecurity. Without the relationship, I would have still ended up in a damaging situation of some sort, with my insecurity driving me. In hindsight, I wish I had done a lot of things differently. Through the knowledge, wisdom, and experience I've gathered over the years, I can now see that I made a lot of irrational and hasty decisions, that were led by my insecurities. I wish I would have been more secure in the love of God and the love for myself, which would have helped me make the decision not to have an abortion. I also wish the people around me—my support system, would not have reflected fear and judgement, but the love of God I know today. The God I have come to know, has a love that is never circumstantial, and an opinion of us that is cemented in His sacrifice and grace—it doesn't ever change. To this day, when a young lady, affiliated with the church or beyond, turns up pregnant, I treat her with love, dignity, and respect, knowing she's doing something I could not. I ask about the date of her baby shower, what she needs, and how her support system is helping her. I'm often met with wide eyes, because many of these young ladies expect that, as a pastor, I'm perfect and disappointed in them.

"Honey, I don't have a foot to stand on. You're my hero," is what I'd like to say to these women. I always want to be the one to encourage them—to be what I didn't have and what I wished for, but knew I wouldn't get. I typically push them to continue their education and follow their dreams, knowing that their journeys, possibly as single parents, will be challenging enough. They should never have to live down other people's opinions.

I remember the first time I spoke of having an abortion at a women's service; these women's jaws were down to their knees. It was the first time I had publicly spoken of it, after feeling like it was absolutely necessary because there were so many women in the room hiding from themselves. Their hiding was easy to see. After you struggle with something and receive freedom and healing from it, it's as if an internal radar is implanted. When insecurity shows its face, you see it immediately. After prayer and prompting from the Lord, I decided to tell my parents, knowing it was critical to my healing, and that eventually, my experiences would be used to help others. Confession is essential and very much a part of the healing process. You cannot receive healing while hiding your secrets. For many of us, our secrets have helped cement our shame and memories. I am not one to advertise telling any and every one things that are very sensitive, but as you heal, you will be led to confess to the right people, at the right time.

My father cried and seemed depressed for a little while after I told him. I believe he felt like he'd failed me. But the confession freed me to speak on what I'd already been freed from, long before ever telling a soul. My transparency broke walls. I could see people melting in their seats as they began to come clean with themselves. After the service, several women, all regular church goer's, confided in me regarding very deep and private matters. Some had been in elicit affairs outside of their marriage, or in someone else's marriage. Some were caught in a cycle of having multiple sex partners. Then, there were those who'd had one or multiple abortions. Some cried in my lap, while others let out sighs of relief at finally being able to admit what they'd been keeping a secret. No matter the confession, the commonality was that you would have never been able to tell their method of supplementing, secrets, and shame, by simply looking at them. They'd all found ways to appear to have it all together.

Since then, I've talked to many women who had come to me, contemplating abortion. My sister was one of them. She was in tears after finding out that she was pregnant with my niece, and dreaded telling my parents. This is when I revealed to her that I'd had an abortion. Her eyes were as wide as quarters. Through my transparency, I was able to help save the life of my niece, along with many other babies. It wasn't my experience that made it possible to save them, it was my transparency. It was my willingness to shed my secrets, get naked, and show my scars. Your healing has either not started, or isn't complete, until you're ready to be transparent.

TRANSPARENCY

"One time... That's all it took me to open my mouth and share what I'd held in for so long, thinking it would cause people to see me differently. But in speaking up, I found the courage to accept myself, whether or not anyone else ever did."
- Teachia Turrentine

If you notice, I've spent more chapters diagnosing and describing insecurity, than I have telling how to fix it. The is because if I couldn't convince you that there was a problem, you would not believe that you need the cure. The cure is the easiest part to understand. The problem has rooted itself in the fibers of your being. It has become as much a part of you as your name, social security number, momma and daddy. To you, it looks like you. If you cannot be convinced that it's not you, you also cannot be convinced that the cure is something you need. If you are one who has gotten this far by reading from beginning to end, but still feel you've lived free of insecurity, I challenge you to start over, from the front cover, to this very sentence. If you're a rarity who has lived free of insecurity, or has somehow made it to a place of freedom long before reading this, I encourage you to keep reading. Perhaps I can provide you with some things to pass on to others, so they can get to where you are.

The call for transparency is not necessarily a challenge to be transparent with others. If you are unable to be transparent with yourself first, transparency with others will be misguided, and may potentially be used against you. When we haven't taken the time to self-evaluate and reflect within, we tend to go to those who we are in relationship with, most of which reflect our own conditions, and vent or share parts of our lives that should only be reserved for people who are positioned to help and encourage us. Our secrets become the topic of gossip and negative conversations among people who are supplementing their own insecurities. By the time our stories get back to our ears, they have so many exaggerations and fabrications, that we look and feel three times worse than when we told them. Furthermore, your change may consist of you never telling anyone besides yourself. There is this common thought that, "being real," includes telling all of your business. Please don't adopt this belief. You are not fake for choosing what to share with others. As long as you have come to terms with yourself, you will eventually be able to assess the need to share your secrets with others. "Being real," consists of your ability to be transparent with yourself and God. If it stops there, you are real enough.

Transparency is the ability to self-evaluate and assess your thought-process and internal makeup. It is the ability not to act or cover up what is at the core of your heart, whether good or bad. It is denial free. If you are in denial, it is the ability to be able to check your heart and motives, and at least ask, "Am I in denial?" It is you being 100% honest with yourself. This is why I have had you journal throughout the book. Each *Journal Moment* is an appeal for you to recall, release, and connect with how you think and feel. Now would be a good time to go back and read some of the things you've written. Using these feelings and desires, you should be able to, at least, start to see yourself. By looking at your current state of mind, you can begin to feel yourself, know yourself, and assess where you are and where you truly want to go. In order for transparency to be possible and effective, you have to include God in this process. Even with the greatest willingness and ability to see yourself, without God, you will miss something, and that "something" is a vital piece of our healing, that has been buried or concealed from us.

Journal Moment

Be transparent with yourself. Voice or admit some things that you have been unable to up until this point in time.

LETTING GOD IN

"Letting God in is a decision. Not always easy... Sometimes it's a brawl between pride, and what you KNOW is true. Sometimes we're wedged so deeply in fear and shame, and other gunk, that parting our parched lips to ask for Him feels unnatural. Do it. The refreshing water of His affirming words, and the anchoring love that He freely gives, results in sweet liberty...Promise! Besides, He's enthralled by you. He won't turn you away." - Jessica Rushton

I have heard many people say, "God is such a gentleman. He'll never force Himself on you." But the true nature of who He is, is a father and a steward. He stewards our lives with such care, tenacity, and intention. He is able to take every part of our lives, and make them benefit us in the long run. Much of our mistakes involve Him sitting back, waiting for us to tire ourselves out and realize that another option exists. Most of us end up where we are, as a result of ignoring His leading and our God-given instincts. After we've had enough of ourselves, we become open to what has always been the best option— GOD.

Letting God in, simply begins with fellowship and continuing to be transparent with Him. After leaving the relationship that I've very candidly spoken of, I came to God so open and wounded. For the first time in my life, I found myself saying things in prayer to God that I would have never said before. Every emotion and feeling surfaced, and I would express feelings of anger, loneliness, frustration, rage, and whatever else was on my heart. It was in those moments of laying on my bedroom floor, talking to God the same way I am to you right now, no fanfare, no "please" and "thank you's," just raw, real me, that I came to realize that was all He'd been waiting on. Our conversations, not prayers, became something real, that I looked forward to. They were therapeutic and healing to my heart. I had always believed something like this was not possible, because of who I thought I was. As I continued talking to God every day, the acceptance I felt, became the thing that kept me coming back.

This is what it means to let God in. It's when you keep coming back, consistently, and repeatedly, daily, in whatever capacity, giving Him your time, attention, and heart. When you come, you are bringing the real you. While there, you are asking and receiving. You are believing, or at least asking Him to help you believe. You are not praying around things or hiding who you are. It's pointless. He already knows anyway. Honestly, it would be better for you to go into prayer and say, "God, I know that 'this' or 'that' is wrong and isn't what you want for me, but I'm just not ready to let it go," rather than going to Him, twiddling your thumbs and talking around the "elephant in the room." Letting God in, is the ability to say, "God, I am scared out of my mind," or, "God, I am so insecure. I don't like who I am," or, "God, I hate her dirty guts." Some of my prayers have been so inappropriate according to man's standards. I've gone into prayer and called more people inappropriate names, like "fart lips," than one should be allowed to. But when you understand that it's a safe place, free of judgment or criticism, you let it rip. It's not that direction and correction don't exist in this place; God has asked me to shut up more times than I can count. It's just that it flows from a nature you trust, knowing you're accepted and loved. Even "Shut up, Shaunee," is received with love and gratitude. This is truly what Social Security is: being *social* with God and finding *security* through fellowship. No monthly paycheck from the government comes close to this type of provision.

Journal Moment

What does letting God in consist of for you? How have you kept Him out knowingly, and unknowingly? Are you ready to let Him in? If not, why? If yes, what are you willing to do differently to accomplish this? Honesty is key.

TRUTH

"Truth is the reality/realm of us being placed in Christ in heaven. Truth shines light on a person. You know when you're in truth when your freedom is more about the One who freed you, rather than freedom itself."
- Mitchell "BJ" Jones, Jr.

After several instances of me talking, God began to talk back. It isn't that He wasn't talking before, my ear just wasn't trained to hear a voice that I'd never entertained with the right mindset. The acceptance I now felt, produced a feeling of love. Now that I felt loved, the thought that God would not speak to me, no longer existed. I'd been raised under the notion that God reserved His voice for those holy enough to hear it. The truth is, His voice is easier to hear when love has removed the fear. For a while, His voice consisted of removing my shame and condemnation. He spoke to every area that needed to be built up. He didn't deal with my failures or the presence of sin that may have still existed. He dealt with who He'd created me to be. My mind began to be renewed. As it was being renewed, I began to display the will of God for my life, as reflected in Romans 12.2, "Do not conform to the pattern of this world, but be transformed by the renewing of your mind. Then you will be able to test and approve what God's will is–his good, pleasing and perfect will" *(NIV)*. As my mind changed, so did my life and the fruit it bared.

Every lie in my life began to be systematically exposed. Truth is a process. God feeds us one bit of truth at a time. To do it all in one step, would be too much for some of us to handle. We would end up feeling as if we hadn't made any progress at all. The idea that you will one day "arrive," is a setup for condemnation. You will never arrive to a place where battles don't come. I have literally been on a never-ending journey of truth from the moment I gave my heart to God. He has used different times and seasons to show me a belief that I'd adopted, how it was false, and how it had affected me. Even now, I am ever-aware of the growth that still needs to happen in me. Our ability to understand this, is part of our dependability and trust in Him. He who has begun a good work in us, will perform it until the day of Jesus Christ. *(Phil. 1.6)* Arrive... HA! Not anytime soon! It's a lifelong journey that you are free to take with peace and confidence in Him. Every truth He reveals, will be done in His way. Remember, He's a father and a steward. He's also a bit of a magician. He makes magic out of your life. It happens when you least expect it.

I will never forget the day I truly realized how my religious experiences had caused me much shame and displacement. It was my first time going to a professional counselor. Three months before this day, I was in my kitchen cleaning and washing dishes when, all of a sudden, I had a brief vision. I was in my elementary school classroom, seated in one of the old desks, with the wooden lift top. I was my current age, but confused as to why I was there. As I looked around, I could hear the sound of something falling, like woodchips on a hard surface. As I looked down, I realized that the sound was coming from something falling from my face, onto the desk. When I looked up, it was scales peeling from my eyes. I knew then, that God was getting ready to reveal truth to me, and that I was getting ready to go through a season of learning. Up until this point, I didn't think I needed a counselor. I felt counselors were for people with "real" issues. How self-righteousness of me! Who doesn't have real issues?

Let me dispel this myth right now. In this day and age, counseling and therapy have a stigma attached to them, especially among the African American community. The stigma is that these methods of intervention are for "crazy" people. We tend to label people who utilize counseling, therapy, and psychiatry services. I believe these services are useful for most people, especially those without any religious bias, since some of our issues are more natural and practical. Religion sometimes has a way of sensationalizing, or making natural matters spiritual, thus keeping us stuck and unable to see truth. At the suggestion of my and my husband's church overseer, I, like most of the ministers under him, had gone to see a counselor for more of a therapeutic approach, as a safe place to vent and relieve stress. Only, somewhere in the course of talking about things, God's magic started working. As I tried to stay on others, the questions slowly began to go back to why I thought the way I did. I'd say one thing, and the response of the counselor would be, "So why do you think you feel that way?" I'd say something else, and the response was still, "So why do you think you feel that way?" After this happened many times, it began to cause the layers to be peeled back. Eventually, the counselor got to my childhood and my experiences with God and church. She looked me in my eye and said, "This is where all of your shame comes from." I left her office, popped a peppermint in my mouth, got in my car, and during the 30-minute drive home, I cried nonstop. As a matter of fact, I cried for a week.

"Oh my God. I am jacked up! God, how do I fix this?" I asked.

You see, this is what truth initially feels like. The goal of truth is freedom, but initially, truth doesn't always feel like truth. It can tend to feel like it's taking something from us, but in reality, it's giving something to us. It confronts lies that have kept us in chains; some of which we have come to depend on, because they protect our comforts and false realities. Once truth is accepted, it becomes the pathway to a new reality, which gives life beyond what our chains would allow us to see. Never fight truth—fight to be free from anything in your life that opposes it. When truth destroys our false reality, we are often left reeling for stable ground to hope and believe in again. It can feel like our security has been taken, but after we receive it, it produces freedom. It points us in a sure direction. But a lie will always produce the opposite of truth; it'll lead you to bondage. The same way you can tell truth by its fruit, you can spot the presence of a lie by the bondage it produces.

Journal Moment

What truth(s) have you seen or began to see, that you believe only God could have shown you? How do you believe it will or has changed your life? What feelings, thoughts, and emotions, does this truth cause you to have?

IDENTITY

"In our world and society, identity is often measured by our material possessions. But as believers, our identity is our reflection of the one who possesses us." - Timothy Dye, Sr.

As truth is presented, and lies, some of which have been there as long as you can remember, are removed, you will begin to become open to the possibility that much of what you thought about God and yourself was wrong. As you begin to view God differently, you will begin to view yourself differently. It becomes a hand-in-hand operation. You cannot behold your Creator and see all He is, the one who formed and shaped you before you were even thought of, and remain the same. We are the greatest reflection of who He is. As we fellowship with Him, absent of fear or condemnation, it frees us to be corrected and shown things that we would not be able to see, in a state of deception.

I began feeling as if a human transplant had been done in me. My mind was being renewed *(Rom. 12.2)*. I'd spent years thinking there was nothing special about me. I felt the things that were viewed as special, all came from my own efforts, most of which were artificial. I had never been able to connect to things that were real signs of who God had made me to be, because the things I was using to sustain me are the things that had my focus. They blinded me from seeing things about myself that were unique, original, and valuable. They had always been there, the same as yours have. They are things about you that stand out, but in our insecurity, we view them as mediocre or average. Insecurity also keeps us stagnant and unable to view these attributes as resources we're meant to capitalize on. I had influence, persuasion, and leadership abilities that had all gone untapped. I had charm and whit that I was using for the wrong reasons. I was blind to my call, purpose, and the true capacity of my gifts. Artificial things keep us from seeing and appreciating what is real. You see it, but you don't see it with eyes of truth.

Let me make something clear: we are not to confuse our call and purpose with identity, doing so is simply another means of supplementing. Though our call and purpose remain the same, what they entail, can change from season to season. One day, you could be running a corporation, and the next, you could be doing oil changes for a living. One day, you could be ministering to thousands of people, and the next you could be a stay-at-home mom. All of this can be done with the same call and purpose, but different details. Our identity is never found in what we do; it's found in God. We are His, always and forever. Once you understand this, you are free to explore how He has crafted you to reveal Him in the earth. Our identity is meant to reveal Him. Believing it's meant to reveal you, positions you to possibly fight what He has purposed for your life. Sometimes, the revealing of God in our lives includes us being inconvenienced and uncomfortable. Those of us looking to be revealed, have failed to identify with Him.

God had given me eyes of truth, and I began to see who I truly was through fellowship with Him. As the knowledge of who I was began to change, my actions began to change. My relationships and associations began to change. The things I did with my free time began to change. The way I sang changed. The way I viewed things I used to supplement with, changed. And people, oh my gosh, people changed so much to me. I began loving people I couldn't stand before. I realized that, even at their worst, it was never really them I had an issue with, it was myself. I didn't like me. When you don't like yourself, it's hard to determine if people are really the issue. Our perception is muddied by our view of ourselves. I began to have compassion on others. I started forgiving people who had manipulated and abused my kindness and innocence. After coming out of my toxic relationship, I entered into a business deal with two men from church, one of which I'd grown up with. I had stellar credit, in the 800's. They doctored up documents with my credit and ran up over $220,000, using my name and information. I had to file for bankruptcy, but this had been another way I had tried to supplement. I blatantly ignored direction from the Holy Spirit, who sent my uncle, an unbeliever, to my house the night before I signed paperwork. While in conversation, he strongly urged me not to enter into an agreement with these men; yet, because he was an unbeliever, my religious nature caused me to miss the truth that God would use anyone or anything to keep us from harm. I was so legalistic and ignorant. It was hard for me to believe that anyone who regularly attended church or who I knew, would harm me. It was such a hard lesson. It taught me never to lean to my own understanding again, and to rely on the voice of the Holy Spirit. After identity came, I forgave even them. Everything about me changed. The people who had benefited from my insecurity, didn't like the change.

They began asking me, "Who do you think you are?" I love when people ask, "Who does he/she think they are?" People who are secure never ask that question. It was their way of trying to keep me in place or knock me down a peg, but it was too late. I'd already gotten wind of who I was, and I was hooked. I could not be intimidated back into a place of mediocrity. My changes would remain, because they represented a new person. There was nothing temporary about it, and furthermore, I was starting not to care what people thought about me. I cared what the right people thought—those who genuinely loved me, but it was a healthy care. It was the kind we need as individuals—the kind that helps you accept correction and constructive criticism. These types of relationships build you and are as responsible for your growth, as the ones that were responsible for your stagnation.

As I remained transparent, let God in, and accepted truth, my mind continued being renewed. It became an ongoing process. People say that God won't share us, and that it is all or nothing with Him, and that's true for certain points in our lives according to His specific instruction, but what He will do, is love and fellowship with the parts of you that you give Him. He will not share space, nor will He plant truth with a lie. One immediately cancels the other. You cannot have the truth of a thing, believe it, and also believe a lie about the same thing. When we remain in fellowship with things that take our affection and focus, God will not combat these things, to have that area. There is no such thing as forced entry with God. Before He can live in His designated space, He will ask you to cooperate with Him while He removes everything that is foreign. Oh yes, this will cost you supplements that you LOVE, but you will quickly see that there is no comparison to what HE provides. This is the nature of insecurity: you can always identify it by what it NEEDS to survive. You'll know that you're no longer insecure, when what you view as necessary for your survival, is what flows from God.

Be prepared for the change. Be prepared to hold on to nothing. All things should be able to be discarded, as you realize they've caused you harm. The process of God implanting identity, is very much about removal, prior to implantation. He clears a space, so that He can fill it with the right thing. You'll begin to value things you've misunderstood or looked over. Your ability to find value in yourself, will have just as much to do with God, as it does with you. When your understanding of who He is has been changed, you will begin to understand your importance. One day I looked up and said, "God, seemingly the most elusive, out of reach person in the world... certainly the most talked about and desired in some form, cares about me." I drove down the road, baffled. The most famous of them all, cared about me. The reality of His importance, in comparison to what I'd believed to be my unimportance, transformed my mind. When people asked, "Who does she think she is?" I would say to myself, "Someone I never imagined."

Journal Moment

Who do you truly believe you are as a person? How much of your identity is founded in God? How much of it is founded in external things? How much of your opinion of yourself comes from people? How much of your opinion of yourself do you believe needs to change? How much of it has already changed for the better?

WALKING IN THE SPIRIT

"The Spirit walk is one of love, or it's not a Spirit walk at all. It's a journey of love that both kills us, and makes us alive." - Tatila Harris

Of all the steps to take in receiving the cure, walking in the Spirit may be listed last, but will become your most valued step in finding and remaining secure in your identity. As I mentioned before, we are only as secure as we are connected to God and ourselves. At the source of insecurity, lies fear, inadequacy, and anxiety. Once we find freedom through a new revelation of God and ourselves, it is essential that we remain connected to the source of life provided to us here in the earth.

Since we are human and wrapped in flesh, everything that is perishable, can be seen in our flesh. Death, disease, disability, all attack our flesh. It is the same spiritually. Everything that leads to us perishing, or to the death of who we are, can be found in our flesh. Insecurity is a work of the flesh. It needs our fleshly desires and fleshly supplementing to survive. In order to remain in control over the most unpredictable part of us, our flesh, we must remain in fellowship with the Spirit.

"For what the Law could not do, weak as it was through the flesh, God did: sending His own Son in the likeness of sinful flesh and as an offering for sin, He condemned sin in the flesh, 4 so that the requirement of the Law might be fulfilled in us, who do not walk according to the flesh but according to the Spirit. 5 For those who are according to the flesh set their minds on the things of the flesh, but those who are according to the Spirit, the things of the Spirit. 6 For the mind set on the flesh is death, but the mind set on the Spirit is life and peace, 7 because the mind set on the flesh is hostile toward God; for it does not subject itself to the law of God, for it is not even able to do so, 8 and those who are in the flesh cannot please God. 9 However, you are not in the flesh but in the Spirit, if indeed the Spirit of God dwells in you. But if anyone does not have the Spirit of Christ, he does not belong to Him. 10 If Christ is in you, though the body is dead because of sin, yet the spirit is alive because of righteousness. 11 But if the Spirit of Him who raised Jesus from the dead dwells in you, He who raised Christ Jesus from the dead will also give life to your mortal bodies through His Spirit who dwells in you. 12 So then, brethren, we are under obligation, not to the flesh, to live according to the flesh— 13 for if you are living according to the flesh, you must die; but if by the Spirit you are putting to death the deeds of the body, you will live. 14 For all who are being led by the Spirit of God, these are sons of God. 15 For you have not received a spirit of slavery leading to fear again, but you have received a spirit of adoption as sons by which we cry out, "Abba! Father!" 16 The Spirit Himself testifies with our spirit that we are children of God, 17 and if children, heirs also, heirs of God and fellow heirs with Christ, if indeed we suffer with Him so that we may also be glorified with Him" (Rom. 8.3-17, NASB).

Our mental and spiritual transformation can be undone through a lack of maintenance. We are surrounded by external influences, and overstimulated through day-to-day living. Work, family, social media, television, and visuals surrounding us, are constantly battling for our attention. When we stimulate our flesh, our flesh lives and rules us. Wherever our flesh rules, it causes death. This is not a physical death, but a spiritual one. This is the reason our insecurities thrive and rule us as long as they do. They are being fed daily through fleshly outlets, causing death within us. Who we truly are, is being crucified, while the imposter ruled by insecurity, lives. The only way to kill the imposter, is to fellowship with the Spirit, who knows who we truly are, and speaks truth to us that produces life. It is by the Spirit that we put to death the works of our flesh *(Rom. 8.13)*. As our flesh dies, our Spirit lives, continually giving us life, peace, direction, joy, and purpose. Most importantly, of everything the Spirit speaks to us, it consistently reminds us that we are His—heirs of His kingdom *(Rom. 8.16-7)*. We represent Him in the earth. We have literally been given a Spirit, whose job is not to rule us with fear, but teach us that God is our father *(Rom. 8.15)*. When we are aware that we belong to God, we also recognize that everything God is and has, belongs to us. Living with this understanding, removes the fear and anxiety that once led us away from who we were created to be. Absent the Spirit, we will easily gravitate back to places that feed our carnal nature, and open us up to a life filled with the consequences of fleshly actions.

Let me be clear: walking in the Spirit does not make you exempt from hardship. As a matter of fact, it will often lead you right to it, for a few different reasons: A.) Because you are a solution for it, and/or B.) Because it is a way to develop everything God has invested and expects of you. It becomes a sort of resistance training. I work out 5 days a week. I've found that burning fat and building muscle and definition, is not only done through lifting weights, but through any technique that causes resistance. I can lift weights, but if my selected weight does not challenge me to work my muscles hard, it is not providing what I need to teach them to bear more weight without damage. Becoming defined and toned, is the result of our muscles being challenged through resistance, torn down, then in the recovery stage, built back up even bigger and stronger. The Spirit walk often leads us into things we've tried to avoid. It leads us into unavoidable interaction with people we can't stand. It leads us into seasons where there are more bills than money to pay them. It leads us to seasons involving unruly family members, disrespectful supervisors at work, disappointing news from the doctor, trouble in our marriage, and so on. Our Spirit walk builds resistance and provides definition. Many of us have made the mistake of using things to define us, that are unable to provide definition. The Spirit walk teaches us to trust, as we are being developed. It not only reveals areas of the flesh, but kills them as they are uncovered. The Bible says that our flesh is literally HOSTILE toward God, that it opposes Him, and cannot be subjected to Him. It doesn't say it chooses not to, but that it literally can't! No good thing lives within our flesh. It is the side of us that directly opposes what is good for us. Without a Spirit walk, our flesh is free to lead us.

The Holy Spirit is a gift, given to us by the Father, when Jesus left the earth. While here on earth, Jesus did all of the speaking, leading, teaching and guidance, but upon His leaving, He left the Holy Spirit to function in us, as He had when He was on earth. This is what Jesus said:

"But when he, the Spirit of truth, comes, he will guide you into all the truth. He will not speak on his own; he will speak only what he hears, and he will tell you what is yet to come. He will glorify me because it is from me that he will receive what he will make known to you" (John 16.13-14. NIV).

Walking in the Spirit consists of constantly being fed and led in truth by God. We literally hear and receive what Jesus is saying on a personal level for our lives, daily. Everything that comes to us, is being made known by the Father, for our direction and benefit. It becomes a source by which we depend on to live. We learn to trust its benefit in our lives. Walking in the Spirit does not only consist of hearing, but doing as we are led. It is an internal source that is consistently taking inventory of our strengths and weaknesses, in accordance with God's plans for us. We are never left to depend only on what we can produce. The Spirit's function is to make up the difference by going beyond what our own senses provides for us.

"In the same way, the Spirit also helps our weakness; for we do not know how to pray as we should, but the Spirit Himself intercedes for us with groanings to deep for words; and He who searches the hearts

knows what the mind of the Spirit is, because he intercedes for the saints according to the will of God" (Rom. 8.26-27, NASB).

The beauty of the Holy Spirit is that even though we house Him, we don't control or manipulate Him. He is not following our will, but the Father's. As we continue to fellowship with the Spirit, He prays the will of the Father for us. It is a continual process of becoming. Any desire of ours that is not in line with the Father's, is revealed as we walk in the Spirit. It is essential to walk in the steps that have been ordered for your life in every season, and with every opportunity presented.

The more I began to learn who I was, the more it led me into a secure relationship with God. His voice became very clear to me. I used to think, *God is that you, or me?* I struggled deciphering between His voice, and my own thoughts. However, as my prayer time evolved into very real encounters with Him, He would speak directly to my heart or lead me in ways that were in line with His will for my life. I went from making every decision on my own, to none without Him. Through the reality of my acceptance in Him and His love for me, it became easier to sense Him. His love had, indeed, removed all fear. Without fear present and with love reigning, I was able to rest in the process of becoming more like God.

Walking in the Spirit is not something you try to do. It is not even as intentional as some have suggested through their interpretations of scripture. It is the result of intentionality. When we are intentional about time spent with God, or sacrificing for Him, the result will be a greater connection with Him. As we connect with Him, He uses the Holy Spirit, a gift freely given to us, to communicate with us. Some would describe it as a still, small voice inside, but, sometimes, I have found it to be a loud, small voice. It is gentle, even when correcting or confronting, but it carries authority and the ability to break through thoughts and intellect. It is often difficult for me to describe, as I have learned that God speaks to each of us differently. Yet, because He is the same, His nature is as well. No matter who He's speaking to or who He's leading, His nature does not change. This is why He said His sheep would know His voice *(John 10.27)*. It is unmistakable. With more fellowship, you begin to recognize it when you hear it.

I was in the bathroom, applying a facial mask, which gave me a seafoam green complexion. The same instance happened with both of my daughters when they were two years old. They both walked into the bathroom, saw me with a mask on, and their light-hearted, happy expressions, immediately turned to fear. They both ran and began crying. I would say something along the lines, "It's okay, honey! It's me!" Haven asked, "Momma?" Her face was completely bewildered, as she stood out of harm's way. I smiled and said, "Yes, honey! It's Momma." I gestured for her to come to me for a hug, but she was still afraid of my appearance. I went back and forth for a few seconds with her:

"Momma?" She'd ask.

"Yes, it's me, baby. Come here, honey." I'd say. Until finally, she was smiling and hugging her green-faced momma, knowing that it was, in fact, me. Her comfort, trust, and ability to come to me, depended on her ability to recognize my voice and my nature, not my appearance. God never intended for us to know Him by what we see. What He looks like can change from season to season. God's plans for us often take us to places that cause trouble, hardship, or difficulty, in an effort to save others, produce His will, and build us up. If we depend on appearance, we'll often miss His hand at work. His voice is the work of His Spirit, which dwells within us. It is how we connect to walking in the Spirit. We come to know His voice. He is always loving and admonishing, never forcing. He always provokes us to live the lives provided for us, through His Spirit. There really is no other way to live. As a matter of fact, you cannot choose another way, and live.

Journal Moment

How is your Spirit walk? What areas of it can you improve? Do you believe this is possible? What goals or commitments can you give to it?

NO PRESSURE

Often, with a list or steps laid out, we feel the pressure to use them as a formula of success, or a fool-proof remedy for our issues. However, with God, anything is subject to change. Our relationships with Him are unique and customized to our lives. He may take you down a path of healing that is outside of the order of what I have listed. He may take you to step 4, then 2, then 5, then 1. As you walk in the Spirit, you will see that His ways are sometimes unorthodox and often defy our own understanding. No matter what path He leads you down, there is no pressure! Please, rest in the process. Do not allow anxiety or an immediate desire for results, to overwhelm your peace. Please know that God's intentions are for you to be whole and healed. His desire is to see you thrive. Your job is to know that you are able to do this. Don't let your confidence be stolen from you, and don't give it away either. Constantly re-affirm yourself and say, "I AM ABLE TO DO THIS." I know this sounds like a simple sentence, but it is often not so simple to believe. Much of what we perceive as laziness, complacency, and procrastination, is a result of our unbelief. When we don't believe, it is because we feel our effort will be wasted. Without effort, no steps will result in success. You must start to believe that you can do everything you have told yourself you can't. Without your belief, there is no cure for insecurity.

9

A NEW STANDARD OF LIVING

"I am convinced that the jealous, the angry, the bitter and the egotistical are the first to race to the top of mountains. A confident person enjoys the journey, the people they meet along the way and sees life not as a competition. They reach the summit last because they know God isn't at the top waiting for them. He is down below helping his followers to understand that the view is glorious where ever you stand." -
Shannon L. Alder

What now? Some of you may be wondering. You have all this new information—the quotes, journal notes, and everything in between; yet, you may be thinking: *This is the last chapter and I still don't feel like I have a handle on this. It still doesn't feel simple at all.* On the other hand, some of you may feel like you've finally grasped it all, and are ready to move forward into change. No matter where your confession is, with all you have come to know, you are now accountable. There is a reason why "ignorance is bliss." Not knowing, relieves us of the responsibility of action. The common misconception is that it also relieves us of consequences. It does not. You can still be hurt, hindered, and prevent your evolution, even when you don't know what is causing such consequences. It is, in fact, still causing it. Deciding to continue implementing tactics and coping mechanisms to get by, after you've been made aware, won't feel as good as it did before. Your internal voice and conscience will remind you of the roots of these mechanisms and the damage they cause. It can often seem easier to remain as we are, but when knowledge comes, it brings more of a desire to change, whether or not the change is easy. We want to be better. The thought that *it just doesn't seem simple,* is correct. It's not all that simple, but there are simple parts. The simplest part of it all, is to set your mind on enjoying the journey. Relax, chill, and rest. Just as your insecurities weren't birthed overnight, uprooting them will not be an overnight process. Over the years, layers have constantly been added to your insecurities. Much like the implanting process, detoxing will take time. If we are anxious and try to hurry the process, we miss the opportunity to grow and learn much of what we will need, in order to effectively change. The knowledge you've received will not be what changes you, but it'll be your ability to apply the knowledge to your life and journey, in whichever ways necessary. Your process of evolution may be similar to mine, but it will not be mine. Again, RELAX. Rest assured your change is possible and inevitable, if it's what you desire.

As mentioned before, you still have the power of choice. You will learn that this process of healing will require a new standard of living. This standard will consist of making daily choices, meant to produce results and change. Without the right choices, your new found knowledge will go to waste. Your ability to believe in the power of applying what you know, consistently, will help you change internally. There are many individuals who are well informed in their professions. Doctors, lawyers, pastors, personal trainers, etc., all have knowledge that they give to other to help them change. Yet, there are doctors who have bad habits that affect their health, lawyers who break the law, pastors who are hypocrites, and personal trainers who frequent fast food restaurants. This process never boils down to knowledge alone, but also requires will power. You have to want your change, more than your comfort. There will be days where you will be tempted to revert back to old habits, but if you condition your mind for the difficulties that may present themselves, you will be able to overcome them, having been prepared.

Whenever people are equipped with the information necessary to change, but still fail to, it is an issue of mind conditioning. Every dysfunction in our lives, goes back to what we think. As we think in our hearts, so will we be. Mind conditioning is vital in transformation. I remember struggling to make changes in an area. I went to God for months about it, until one day, while whining about it, God spoke to me and said, "Your problem is that you're waiting for this to be easy." I nearly stopped my car in the middle of the road, as I let the truth of this statement sink into my spirit. I had not thought about it this way. As I self-reflected on this truth, it resonated. I had been thinking— well, hoping, that one day my challenge would no longer be a challenge. I subconsciously believed one day I would wake up and BAM! No more struggle! Whether we would like to admit it or not, most of society hopes or believes this way. We think that, eventually, we'll outgrow certain guilty pleasures, making them easy to let go of. The truth is, they have become very much a part of how we have learned to endure life. Letting go of them can feel like we are letting go of us. In certain cases, it can feel like death or the loss of a beloved friend or family member. If you do not begin to condition your mind now, concerning the truth of your process, you will give up when it gets hard or when feelings that have been suppressed for years, begin to surface. You will quit, either before you get started, or right in the middle of change. Without constant mind conditioning, you *will* quit.

But, again, walking in the Spirit, means you're not doing this alone. You always have help within you, championing your growth.

"No temptation has overtaken you but such as is common to man; and God is faithful, who will not allow you to be tempted beyond what you are able, but with the temptation will provide the way of escape also, so that you will be able to endure it" (1 Cor. 10.13, NASB).

Much of your mind conditioning will help you endure internal battles that consist of negative thinking and temptation to give in to old ways. The one thing I have found about temptation, is that it is easier to endure than the way of escape. Temptation feels most natural when our flesh is alive. It's the way of escape God chooses for us, that is usually the hardest to endure, as it often defies our fleshly nature. Our escape is typically connected to the opposite reaction of what comes natural to us. The temptation feels like home, while the way of escape feels like we've been dropped off on the side of the road, in a foreign country. Yes, my friend, we are enduring the way of escape, not always the temptation. As you change, the temptations may still come, but the way of escape begins to feel more like home—more like the safest and most natural place for you to reside.

As you walk in a new standard of living, you will find that life will take on many new changes, as a result of your mind being continuously renewed. Your new mindset and the decision not to revert to old ways of supplementing your insecurity, will begin to demand that things birthed in your old mindset, change or be removed. You will begin to feel uncomfortable, discontent, and unsettled with things that used to feel perfectly normal. You will find that settling into your "new normal," will only come once you have confronted, purged, and restructured areas of your life, in order to maintain your new growth. There will be many different areas for you to tackle. Here are a few to prepare yourself for.

YOUR NEW SUPPLEMENT

"Finally, be strong in the Lord and in his mighty power."
- Ephesians 6:10, NIV

Up until this point, supplementing has been discussed in terms of the negative ways it affects us, pertaining to our insecurities. The flip side of this is that, no matter how much we come to love and understand ourselves, we are never too good to not need God. He is ultimately what makes up the difference and eternally satisfies every deficiency we could ever carry. He is forever the answer to every question and calamity we could ever face. Where we used to turn to external things to meet our need for security, we now remain secure in Him. Your new standard of living will begin and end in remaining in your place of trust and dependency on God. If at any time you stray from this, you open yourself up to pulling from external sources again. For those who choose not to rely on God at all, your hope remains in yourself and others. In choosing not to rely on God, you ultimately gamble your sanity and peace of mind. Remain rooted in God, knowing there is no guessing and/or gambling. He does not misdiagnose our conditions. When administering the cure, He does not miss. He targets the area, and with our cooperation, removes everything hindering His plan for our lives. From now on, He is your supplement. He is the rock you run to. There is no other option—no other way. Everything else in life that we enjoy, is only possible because we have security in Him. Are you sad, lonely, afraid, hopeless, tempted? No matter what you feel, GO TO GOD. If it doesn't go away, GO TO GOD AGAIN! If it's still there, GO TO HIM! Don't ever stop going, even when you fail...GO! This is your new standard.

PEOPLE

"I have insecurities of course. But I don't hang out with anyone who points them out to me." - Adele

People, people, people. I hate to even have to address people in this matter, but I must. Why do people matter so much? They are a large part of what makes insecurity possible. The "people factor" is something that only highlights what's there. As you continue making changes, you will see that your relationships will also change. Revelation, maturity, and growth, will always show the true nature and value of your current relationships. Relationships founded on artificial, superficial, and supplemental natures, don't typically evolve as you evolve. We tend to outgrow them and become unable to bring them along with us as we walk our new journeys. If these relationships have proven to be toxic and we try remaining attached to them as we grow, they will either hinder our continued growth, or stop it all together. Conversations, activities, and other things that used to seem normal in these relationships, will now feel like a stretch or a forced effort. We won't view these relationships the same, because we are now equipped with the understanding of the damage they cause.

Let me be clear, breaking off or redefining some of these relationships will not be easy. Do you hear me? Doing this, may be the hardest thing you have ever had to do. There will be friends, family members, and love interests who have known you as you were, for a very long time—maybe all of your life. Some of these relationships will be with people who have ONLY known the broken, insecure you. Please hear me: the truth is, some of these people greatly benefited and capitalized on your brokenness. Some of them were largely responsible for the added layers of damage through their manipulation, selfishness, abuse, and diminishing of your worth. Those of us who really struggled with self-love, will find that many of our relationships, directly reflect how we felt about ourselves. We will find that many of them represent us settling for far less than what we are worth.

Just so you know, your worth is invaluable. It is not always that people are bad or dead-set on hurting you. As you change and become more sensitive to the Spirit, you will begin to feel a lot of compassion and understanding for people you used to hate. God spoke to me one day and said, "People will never value something in you that they don't value in themselves." I began to see that if a person looks at a 50-dollar bill and thinks it's worthless, when you come along, stocked with 50-dollar bills, they will also think yours are worthless. When people don't understand the value, or purpose of a thing, they will, without a doubt, misuse or abuse it. When we connect with other people who are suffering from low self-esteem, a lack of confidence, insecurity, jealousy, and negativity, they typically only find value in things that help them supplement how they feel. These things are usually artificial. It isn't that they don't want to see your worth, they just can't. Their current level of understanding makes it impossible to make true assessments.

As your eyes are opened to the truth of these relationships, you may be led to lessen, or break your connection with them all together. PEOPLE WILL NOT LIKE THIS. You may be accused of "thinking you're better," "acting funny," being withdrawn, or any number of labels that people with limited understanding resort to. What you need to do, is refuse to defend yourself. Let them run their lips as much as they want. Anyone running and telling you everything that's being said about you, also needs to be cut off. If the relationships are truly worth having, a little time apart will not hurt. Do not be afraid to ask for time. Do not be afraid to decline invites, or to spend evenings home alone. Though it may be a lonely time for you, you cannot look at it as you being alone. *YOU* are with you, spending time with yourself, getting to know yourself. The isolation that getting to know yourself requires, is removing everything else begging for your attention and fellowship. You have to look at this like a new love interest you are pursuing. When you first meet someone who peaks your interest, you want to see where this interest leads. You invest a lot of time and attention into getting to know the person, developing a bond. You owe the same time and attention to yourself. Set aside time to spend with God and yourself. Our discovery of God, becomes a discovery of ourselves. Anyone or anything that gets in the way of this discovery, is not worth it.

For people who cannot be avoided, such as family, or those in environments you must frequently visit, you have to implement boundaries. You can begin to redefine your interaction with people. A change of conversation and commitment to things you used to do without much thought, is a good way of saying, "Hey! There's a new sheriff in town!" You can gently, yet firmly begin to put your foot down. Eventually, even the most undiscerning, aloof, and stubborn of them, will begin to see that you're not the old you anymore. If they decide to leave because of it... BUH-BYE. BON VOYAGE. ARRIVEDERCI. SAYONARA. ADIOS. You get the point? Don't be afraid of people leaving. Sometimes their departure is required, for your entrance into a greater place.

I can assure you that as you grow and become secure, you will attract new relationships that carry healthier connections. You will not be without meaningful relationships. You will, however, find that you may have less of them than you did unfruitful ones. Natural, quality things are harder to come by, than those that are artificial. Think about the difference in processed and packaged foods, as opposed to fresh produce and organic foods. Things that are natural and better for you, cost more. The quality of these foods is better because they lack artificial, unhealthy ingredients, that make up most processed items. When something is pure and organic, not only does it carry all the necessary nutrients to feed you, but also to cure you. My most valuable and necessary relationships are not those I picked or pursued; God put each of them in my life at the right time. All of them evolved organically, of course with my commitment, but not with anything artificial or forced.

After coming out of the unfruitful relationship I was in, I reeled for a while. I went on a few dates with people I knew were also not good fits for me. I wasn't ready to be alone and face the process of dealing with what I'd come out of. One day in prayer, God spoke to me and said, "Just give me one year." I was like, "Um, huh?" I'd heard Him very clear and I knew what He meant. This is when everything changed. There is something about when God speaks to our hearts. All it takes is one sentence, phrase, or suggestion, and the entire meaning and conversation is downloaded into your understanding. You know exactly what He means. You can examine His tone, and feel His heart. He was asking me not to date anyone for a whole year. Jesus. I was young, spry, and cute. I didn't like anyone in particular, but I still liked that people liked me. My insecurity depended on that type of attention. Yet, here He was, asking me to give it up. I was being loved on, and that love compelled me. I set out to follow God and walk in the Spirit. For an entire year, with a few close calls, I did not date anyone. I didn't go to the movies, dinner, not even for coffee, with any male suitors. It even got to the point where I stopped giving out my phone number and accepting phone calls. I began to sense the distractions. I was growing so much because of my obedience. I didn't want ANYTHING to jeopardize that. I remember the day "the year" ended. August 4, 2004. I woke up and said, "Well God, I made it." I felt so happy—so proud of myself. I wasn't even itching to go on a date. I wasn't perched and ready to go. I was content. Later that day, I went to an outside concert in Detroit, where I had to sing. A gentleman I used to date said, "Hey! Remember that guy I had told you about a long time ago? Well he's here. I want you to meet him." He left and returned with a guy sipping on a fountain drink.

"Shaunee, I want you to meet Gayle Brannan," he said. Just like that, I met my husband, a year to the day I had set out on the journey to meet myself and God. This thing is realer than you think.

Journal Moment

Take inventory of your current relationships. What are the pros and cons of each of them? How many of them need to be redefined? How many of them need to be cut off completely? What are the feelings, emotions, and attachments to these relationships? Are any of these emotions and attachments signs of supplementing? What steps can you take to implement boundaries, break ties, or take time a part?

FORGIVENESS

"True confidence is not about what you take from someone to restore yourself, but what you give back to your critics because they need it more than you do." -
Shannon L. Alder

Forgiveness is a touchy subject for a lot of people, but it is such an essential part of the process of healing and of life itself. A person who is unable or unwilling to forgive, is one who still stands in need of healing. There is a reason I did not include the topic of forgiveness in the chapter entitled "The Cure." The predominant thought in society is that we forgive so that we can heal. The truth is, no matter how hard we try, we are typically unable to forgive until we are healed. Our ability to forgive is often the result of healing we've received. Without the necessary healing, forgiveness becomes a forced act, with no true change of heart. There are various things that hinder our ability to heal and forgive, and a lack of understanding is definitely one of them. It can be very hard to let something go, when you still do not understand the "why" of it. "Why" keeps many of us hostage to unforgiveness. I wish I could promise you that you become healed when the "why" is answered. For many of us, "why" is never addressed. Even when it is, the answer does not always satisfy the desire to know. When walking with the Spirit, He often targets the "why" areas, and brings a personal truth and revelation about us, not always the offender. There is a reason we get hung up on "why." There is a reason bitterness, anger, and strife is present. He targets the areas of our hearts that are responsible for why these qualities exist in us. We usually think they exist because of what was done to us. The truth is, they are there because of the presence of other qualities that lived in us long before things happened to us. We are often asking the wrong "why." But God, in His goodness, answers our "why's" with the correct answers.

There have been many times that my anger or offense has led me to be unforgiving. I would go to God in prayer, and He would deal with me, not the offender. Here's a little inconvenient truth for you: God does not choose sides between people. He's only on His side. What He's determined to be right or wrong, is the side that He stands with. He has no favorites. Even when standing side-by-side with the worst of the worst, you are still not His favorite. He views us all the same, through eyes of love. This doesn't feel good to those who like "sicking" God on other people. We satisfy our anger and offense with the idea that God is going to pay our enemies back for wronging us. Let me just tell you, I have seen some of my "enemies," people who genuinely mistreated me, prosper right in front of my ticked-off face. Here I was angry, offended, and waiting on repayment, and they were off, in their own world, living life, prospering, NOT THINING ABOUT ME. This is usually how unforgiveness works. You are at a standstill, while the person you're waiting on to "get theirs," is at the carnival. God doesn't want to hinge your ability to forgive, on their cooperation, but on yours. The truth is, most of us have been offenders many times as well. If the notion of God repaying our enemies for us worked, we might find ourselves at the bottom of the same hole we looked forward to seeing our enemies thrown into. You never know what peace or resolve people have made with God. Furthermore, you never really know the truth of why people hurt other people. This is why God says, "vengeance is mine." He is the only one equipped to steward vengeance, and what it's meant to accomplish. God never punishes for the sake of punishment, but always to redirect purpose, potential, and provide grace and love. If we were in charge of vengeance, people would be getting hit with lightning bolts left and right!

One day I went to God regarding an issue of unforgiveness I carried. I had repeatedly asked God to help me. I cried, hollered, and told God it wasn't fair. He must have sensed I was ready to hear truth, because He let me have it. He spoke to me and said, "Shaunee, you're taking it personal." I lifted my head from the carpet where I'd been laying, and I got angry. You have to understand; I had been THOROUGHLY mistreated. Hearing Him speak this to me was offensive beyond words.

"Of course I'm taking it personal!" I screamed. After going off on a rant, I got quiet and He did too—too quiet…for a long time. Then, He must have sensed I was ready to hear more truth, so He said, "You're taking it personal, but it's spiritual. This is a spiritual issue." As I began setting my pride to the side and humbling myself, I began to see the truth. People who walk in the Spirit, do not commit the type of offense I had suffered. There was a serious spiritual deficiency present, which produced bad behavior and poor decisions. I made conclusions about the offense, that made me believe I was the target. The truth was, their lack of spiritual stability was a sign of their own harm. As I received this understanding, I removed myself as the target and was able to see the motive and intention of what had been done. Even in instances where attacks were intended to be personal, understanding that people carry spiritual deficiencies that produce bad behavior, has brought me through many offenses, without anger, bitterness, or unforgivenss brewing inside me. When I stopped taking things personal and viewed them as spiritual issues, forgiveness became easier to give.

You may be thinking: *Okay, I get it. I need to forgive. I want to, but I don't know how.* There are many people who adopt the "just move on mentality." We think that because we've left a person or situation, we're on our way to being over it. You can physically leave a thing, but mentally carry it to your grave. If its fruit still remains, so does its root. As long as the root is there, it's still alive, in you, affecting vital areas of your thinking. The act of forgiveness is the ability to relieve a person of a debt. When you are forgiving someone, you are, in essence, saying, "For the wrong you've done to me, you owe me nothing." I know it sounds simple, but for a lot of us, it's not that simple at all. Many of us have allowed things that were done to us to sit and fester, replaying over and over again in our minds. We often do not like to admit it, but subconsciously, we desire retribution for the wrong done to us. We especially desire retribution, when the "wrong" involves matters of the heart that consist of deception, betrayal, or manipulation. We desire to see our offender feel what we felt in moments of pain, despair, and sorrow. If nothing else, we want understanding and empathy for the wrong we suffered. I haven't held back at all yet, have I? You have to face the possibility that the moment may never come. You may never get an apology, a request for forgiveness, or even an acknowledgement of wrong. You may even find that the person stands stubbornly by their actions. What now? If you hinge your healing on another person's actions, you are setting yourself up for bitterness and death of spirit. Forgiveness does not always mean complete removal of negative thoughts and feelings. It does, however, mean that you are no longer waiting on someone's demise in return for the wrong they've done. It also means that if, by chance, their demise should come, you are not overwhelmed with feelings of joy and satisfaction. Happiness at the expense of someone else's demise, even the one who we believe deserves it, is an inferior quality. Your act of forgiveness frees you to move forward with life. It frees your mind, heart, and spirit, to heal and love without the presence of pain. This cannot be an emotional decision. Trust me, your emotions are alive and well. It will not always feel good at first. As for myself, I picked up the phone to dial a number on several different occasions before I was finally able to leave an "I forgive you" voice message. I would get extremely angry and emotional the minute I heard the phone ringing. After a process of layers being peeled back, I was able to come to terms with why I was so angry, making it possible for me to grasp the understanding of what I needed to let go.

You will find that as you heal and come to terms with some of your poor decisions, the anger and disappointment you feel in yourself, will far outweigh what you may feel toward others. It may take some time to actually see that it's YOU that you're angry with. People and external influences are easy and convenient escapes from taking responsibility. This is why God, in His goodness, often takes us through a process of elimination and forgiveness. Your walk with the Spirit will help heal this area of your life. After we're done forgiving and releasing others, we find that we are, somehow, at the bottom of the "I'm angry" ditch. It is often very hard to forgive ourselves, because we find it hard to believe that we fell into some of the traps we did. There is no condemnation to those who walk after the Spirit, not the flesh *(Rom. 8.1)*. Much of our anger towards ourselves is rooted in condemnation and judgement. We may still feel ashamed because of our actions and poor decisions. For those of us who lived selfishly and hurt others, we often watch the damage we caused them. We feel even worse taking inventory of their pain and, often, their unwillingness to forgive us. It's very difficult to forgive yourself with constant reminders of your poor decisions, but God will help you see the areas of your life that made your failures possible. With exposure to truth, the understanding we receive, makes it easier to forgive ourselves and believe in the newness of who we are. Our greatest failures become beautiful testimonies of our survival and evolution. Your shame becomes your greatest accomplishment in overcoming it!

Your ability to walk in the Spirit will be a large part of your ability to forgive. The truth He gives, creates a pathway for you to let go of things that have held you hostage to negative beliefs. The struggle with strife, vengeance, and unforgiveness, are usually characteristics of people who have been taken advantage of. The helpless feeling of your innocent or naivety being exploited, is one that you'll never forget. You are often left with feeling defensive, which places unrealistic responsibilities on you to protect and defend yourself from future instances. I have learned that no matter how good I am at protecting and defending myself, God is much better. Your best efforts do not come close to His. There is not one thing He misses. As we walk in the Spirit, He keeps our eyes open, steering and directing us. As you learn to trust God, you learn to understand what His responsibilities are, and what yours are. The anxiety associated with proving your worth and demanding respect, becomes unnecessary. You will learn that there is no such thing as "demanding respect." This all goes back to the ability to understand value. People who respect themselves, respect others. How they feel about themselves is easily reflected in their interaction with others. When we work to demand respect from people who don't respect themselves, we are doing nothing other than requesting behavior modifications. In essence we're saying, "Don't change how you feel about me, but change how you treat me." Once you begin to learn the nature of people and how they operate, you learn not to waste your time on pointless acts. You become less apt to argue, fight, and challenge people who are blind. As you rest in God's ability to keep you, you release toxic feelings—even those concerning your greatest offenders.

God will lead you into the best path for you to forgive. He may lead you to make a phone call, send an email, or have a face-to-face conversation. He may even simply heal your heart, and tell you to move on. No matter what option He gives you, follow Him with all of your heart. Only He knows what it will take for you to accept your freedom, and once free, you will wonder what took you so long.

Journal Moment

Who do you need to forgive? What are your predominant thoughts concerning forgiving them? Do you believe you can forgive them? What do you need to let go of, in order to do so?

NEW PURSUITS

Now that you are coming in contact with the real you (notice I didn't say "new you," as this is who you've always been, but are just now getting to know), you will find that things that have kept you distracted and pre-occupied will no longer appeal to you, or that you are now strong enough to resist them. You will start recognizing your potential—the potential that has been dormant and untapped. As you come into agreement with God on the things that are in your heart, vision will start to form. The vision will help you to run. You will begin to believe that you can do things you've never imagined, but always hoped to do.

The thing about insecurity, is that it will have you waste time pursuing things that you are either not equipped to do, or that you will not be able to devote all of yourself to, because you are not in touch with all of yourself. We waste time trying to keep up with others, or longing for things that make us appear to be something we're not, while the things we are truly gifted to do, sit on the sidelines waiting on us to realize our ability. Identity positions you to operate out of what you have identified with. As you identify with who God has made you to be, you will be drawn to things that serve your gifts, talent, and purpose. It ignites a fire in you. You start to believe that you can do things you used to talk yourself out of in your insecurity. Procrastination, complacency, quitting, and laziness, are not attributes of people, but attributes of unbelief. When you don't believe in yourself, you feel like effort is a waste of time.

With belief in your heart, things that took you years to complete, are done in half the time. Be open and aware of your new desires and how you're changing. Be willing to give new things a try, and set plans in motion to achieve what is now in your heart. With your new understanding, you are able to hold yourself accountable to accomplish your goals. They will not be easily shaken or disregarded, as before. Your sense of fulfillment and contentment will grow, as you respond to purpose. Ignoring it, will cause the opposite result. Until you respond to purpose, you will not be able to be at peace with God, yourself, or others.

Journal Moment

What are some of the new possibilities and pursuits that you can sense? What steps or plans are you willing to make to obtain them?

AFFIRMATION

"For me, overcoming insecurity for a long time was a combination of becoming more aware of the good qualities that I brought to the table, and embracing the flawed parts of me that honestly needed work. Thinking positively about myself helped me get through the sides of me that seemed difficult to deal with."
- Chantele Gray

Affirmation has been minimized by many people, to consist of the ability to recite anthems, quotes, and pledges to ourselves, in hope of them somehow sticking to our brains. In reality, affirmation is very much an act of agreeing with what we have already come to believe, and encouraging this belief. Affirmation is a vital part of life, both from others, as well as from within. The affirmation we receive from others, is something that encourages us, but not something that we live by. We live by the affirmation that comes from God. People come to affirm what we have already received from God and ourselves. We do not depend on affirmation from others to live, but it works as a strengthening tool for what we already believe. However, the ability to affirm ourselves, is a vital part of remaining encouraged and motivated. God affirms us first, we affirm ourselves next, then lastly, people affirm us. In short, affirmation is the act of saying, "I agree, and I believe."

As you move forward with a new outlook on life, and as new vision, a new sense of purpose, and new goals surface, you will find that old challenges may still arise. There will be times where God will allow you to be tested and tried in ways that seem to have no end. These trials may feel like they're laced with fire. There will be times where you will feel alone, even with God there—you'll feel as if things are just too hard. Women, I'm sure you all can agree, these battles, no matter how big or small, are magnified ten times, when they happen around "that time of the month." Our hormones almost always get the best of us around this time. Adding tests to an already raging fire, makes us crazy! It really is an awful and unfair combination. Men, please give us a free pass. Nod your head, smile, and say, "Okay, dear!" It's best for all of us when this happens. Then, when we come out of it, tell us we acted a fool. When being tested, there will be days where you flat out want to quit. Then, there are days where you do quit. Process stinks!! There were days I vowed not to talk to a soul, shut myself in the house, cut on the TV, eat junk food, and zone out. I quit. I quit with all my might. Quitting never made me feel better, nor did it solve the issue. The next day, I often felt like I was starting all over. Without the proper affirmations to support our goals and visions while being tested, we will not only feel like quitting—we will quit.

To help you affirm yourself, it may be helpful to write down personal affirmations, that are aligned with what God has spoken to you regarding yourself. These affirmations should support your vision and goals. As you grow and change, feel free to add to, or take away from your list. You will know you are not growing and evolving, if you look up a year later, and your affirmations are still the same. View them daily, recite them daily, and pray over them daily. Remember, your ability to remain connected to God and yourself, are so important in remaining secure, confident, and at peace. Without these connections, there will certainly be no joy. Your joy is priceless. I strongly encourage you to eventually come up with your own, but here is a list of affirmations for you to start with. Don't worry about feeling silly. Don't worry if you don't believe all of them yet. Don't worry if it's a struggle to get them out. As you heal, they will flow like water because they will be in agreement with your spirit.

DAILY AFFIRMATIONS

- I am fearfully, wonderfully, and originally made. I am unique in every way.
- I was created in the image of God, I am loved by Him and belong to Him.
- I am being molded and shaped into everything God desires me to be.
- I am not under condemnation, shame, guilt, or regret for past mistakes. I am free to walk in God's love for me. I am no longer held back by my past. I have a bright future.
- In God I live, move, and have my reality.
- I submit to God's will and plan for my life.
- I believe God is directing my steps, providing resources for my vision and goals, and teaching me how to wait with patience, as I trust him.
- I love myself completely. I love every weakness and every strength. I LOVE ME.
- I will not dwell on the things about myself that I do not like.
- I will dwell on my strengths.
- I can do anything I set my mind to.
- I believe in myself. I believe in my ability. I BELIEVE IN ME.

- I walk in hope, joy, peace, and contentment.
- I am worthy of love. I am worthy of being loved. I AM WORTHY.
- I choose to forgive others. I choose to forgive myself.

- I respect myself. I respect others.
- I am growing, evolving, and changing for the better.
- Nothing is too hard for God. Nothing is too hard for me.
- My best days are ahead of me, and I will see them.
- I believe and agree with every word I have spoken.

Recite these daily. Do you hear me? Speak these words EVERY DAY until they are deep within your heart and spirit. They are not idle words. They will bring life, as you agree with the changes you are making. They will help hold you accountable to the process, which I repeat, will not be easy. It's so worth it. You are so worth it. You are gold. You, and maybe even those around you, have yet to see who you truly are. You may have seen pieces, glimpses, or possibilities, but in a place of security, a new reality unfolds beyond what you can hope. No matter how hard it may get, even if you fail some days, keep going! Believe in the power of belief. It will sustain you. Above all, LOVE YOURSELF, knowing you are worth every sacrifice that makes love possible.

NOTES TO REMEMBER

As mentioned before, with this evolution you're experiencing, you will find that new relationships will blossom, some of which have been there all along, but perhaps you've overlooked or took for granted. If you are sincere in asking God for the right friendships and influences, He will send them to you to help cultivate purpose, joy, and your overall well-being. I'd like to leave you with a few notes from someone I have a trusted relationship with. Add these to the notes you've already taken, as reminders of the truth you've already received. When in doubt, read them as gentle reminders of your new truth and standard of life.

- To be totally secure in every area of life, faith in God, and then in oneself, is crucial and foundational.
- Securities challenged on a daily basis:

- o Sometimes some very small things seem huge.
- o Broken routine hinders perceived deadlines.
- o Fear of the reactions of others you know well and how they will respond to situations
- o Fear produces a wrong focus and expectation in life.
- o Fear always thinks the worst; love always thinks the best. So fear is the enemy of love
- FEAR is an emotional energy that seeks to destroy security.
  - o A series of negative thoughts arise when unexpected events or situations take place.
  - o One insecure thought will always lead to another, more serious potential consequence.
  - o Fear is a fire that seeks to destroy everything that is good.
- Sowing and Reaping
  - o A parent who is caught up in fear, will pass the same emotion on to the children.
  - o Young children will reflect the parent in responses to difficult situations.
  - o Anyone who was brought up in a "fear" environment will have to break that assumptive lie.
- Recognize the Source
  - o Overcoming fear begins with recognizing the "why"
  - o Is there a family history?
  - o Has some historic, very serious event taken

    place that causes unhealthy recall?
  - o Is the source demonic? If so it will bring personal accusation against you and your history – mistakes or misdemeanors.
- Dealing with the Situation

144

- Moving faith, then moving confidence
- Renew the mind
- Stay focused.
- If the phone rings, ignore it.
- Praise God for His goodness – speak it out.
- If there is accusation, tell Satan to go.
- Don't look to see if He's gone – He's gone!
- Immediately focus on God in praise and worship.
- Recall God's goodness.
- Continue through the day with the right perceptions.
- Be open – testify to others the bad as well as the good.

- Staying free
  - Don't let the slightest hindrance deflect you from the right focus.
  - If you feel you are getting bound again, set yourself free. You have the Holy Spirit in you!
  - Be prepared to testify to others what you have learned and what God has done.

- Always be ready to help others in the same situation.
  - Tell them something of your own history.
  - Be alongside them, not above them.
  - Empathize
  - Help them to the extent that they can help others, but then not only free them, but help them to know how to remain free.
  - Let them be sure that they can help others. This is important because they will be able to help other people with whom you do not have the relationship.

- Apostle Tony Howson of the United Kingdom

Hi Insecurity. BYE Insecurity.

CONCLUSION

"If you've ever been rescued by God, it is a feeling you will never forget. You do not get up and walk away thinking you are better than others. Oh no, not at all. Instead, the grace you've received, teaches you that you're only better than one person, and that person is who you thought you were."
- Shaunee Brannan

I was six years old and had a really high fever. We'd just left church and I was asleep on the backseat of my dad's Cadillac. My hot face was pressed against the cool leather seats, and I was semi-coherent, drifting in and out of sleep. I could hear my parents talking, and my mom said, "Yeah, her fever is really high. I will give her a bath and some Tylenol when we get home, poor baby." I was sick, really sick, and I felt horrible. My clothes were sticking to my body and I had very little strength. As we pulled into our driveway, my mom hurried the other kids out of the car, and my dad swung my door open. He scooped me up, patted my head on his shoulder, and began to carry me. He carried me all the way from the car, into the house, down the hall, and laid me on my bed. He noticed I was shivering, so he took the blankets to cover me until my bath water was ready. My daddy carrying me was the safest feeling I had ever felt. My fever eventually subsided, and I got better, but that feeling stayed with me. That feeling of safety and love meant everything in the world to me. For months after that, when we were in the car and close to our house, I'd fake like I was asleep and unable to be shaken awake, just so my dad could carry me again. I wanted to replay that feeling over and over again. Eventually I became too big to be carried, but I never stopped being loved and protected, ever. Thirty years later, the feeling still remains.

God wants you to experience this same feeling. When weak, vulnerable, and overtaken, we are unable to fight or get ourselves better, but He loves us so dearly. He wants to pick us up, nurse us back to health, and to help us feel every ounce of love and protection He has for us.

He wants to carry you. No matter what state or condition you're in, good or bad, you are never without the need for Him to carry you. This is the end of the book, but the beginning of something wonderful for you. You have yet to see the full extent of your value and worth. Perhaps you've gotten a glimpse of it, hoped for it, or believed in it, but haven't fully seen it. IT'S YOUR TIME. Open your heart and let

God show you more. The condition of your heart, mind, and will, are God's concerns, and there is nothing that can stop you from thriving, if you set your mind on following God's path for you. You are an absolutely phenomenal flower, waiting to blossom. Fellas, I'm talking to you, too. Don't beat your chest on me, you guys are flowers as well (HA!).

Just in case you haven't heard it fully in the nine chapters, you are not where you come from. You are not your mistakes. You are not your past. You are not your bad decisions. You are not the negative things you've been called, even the ones you've called yourself. You are loved, strong, capable, able—full of purpose. If anything tells you otherwise, tell it to "shut up!" It's only insecurity trying to creep its way into your life. You've come too far and know too much now to let it prosper. You have everything you need within to live free and secure.

We love who you are now and who you are becoming. Thank you for allowing us to go on this journey with you. We believe in you. Now believe in yourself.

Sincerely,

God and Shaunee

Made in the USA
Monee, IL
31 October 2023

45500147R00096